Several decades ago, I traded a commo
name, which 99.99 percent of people
may seem like a little thing to many, bu.
and come to associate our character with our name. In *Living Unafraid*, Grace teaches us about seven different names of God and how his character traits, inherent in each of these names, help us to walk more confidently, courageously, and boldly, exchanging all worry, fear, and anxiety for complete trust in the one who is all that we need him to be. The richness of this devotional study helps the truth of God's character come alive and assures us of our firm foundation for facing life's difficult circumstances.

> **Dr. Michelle Bengtson**, board-certified clinical neuropsychologist; host of *Your Hope-Filled Perspective*; author of *The Hem of His Garment: Reaching Out to God When Pain Overwhelms*

I'm so grateful that Grace Fox faced her own fears to write this devotional study. *Living Unafraid* provides a deep journey into how God reveals himself to us through his names. I was encouraged by the real-life stories Grace shares of people experiencing God's power, presence, and provision to face and conquer fear, even in the face of life's challenges.

> **Dr. Sylvia Hart Frejd**, author, spiritual director, master-certified coach, and coach trainer

If you're looking for a transformational study, it's here! *Living Unafraid* will spark a revival in your heart. You'll discover God to be totally wise, good, and trustworthy. You will learn to embrace his love and care for you. Most of all, you'll experience the security of moving from fear to freedom. I love the way Grace Fox weaves deep biblical truth with contemporary stories, thought-provoking discussion questions, and comforting prayers. Gather your friends and dig into the powerful wisdom in this book.

> **Carol Kent**, speaker and executive director of Speak Up Ministries; author of *He Holds My Hand: Experiencing God's Presence and Protection*

When I want to learn about God, I want to learn from someone who studies God's Word and walks with God to apply and obey his Word. Grace Fox is that person, a scribe on the character and person of God! *Living Unafraid* will be a light to your path toward getting to know God in an intimate and life-changing way.

Pam Farrel, best-selling author of 59 books; coauthor of the Discovering the Bible series; codirector of Love-Wise

Grace Fox's new book is a gem. She thoroughly examines the context and teaching behind seven names of God in the Bible and then helps readers understand what they mean and how God's identity impacts ours. This well-researched book will significantly impact readers and their spiritual formation—and serve pastors and Christian leaders as an important resource to keep on their bookshelves. I recommend it highly.

Janet Holm McHenry, award-winning speaker and best-selling author of 27 books, including *The Complete Guide to the Prayers of Jesus*

Grace Fox writes with a powerful combination of truth, grace, transparency, and vulnerability. I appreciate her close adherence to Scripture and the depth she provides as she unpacks the names of God and how those names reveal unchanging character traits of our loving Father. This book is a great resource for anyone wanting to experience decreased fear, increased faith, and increased intimacy with their Savior.

Jennifer Slattery, host of *Faith Over Fear* podcast

NAMES OF GOD
Living Unafraid

DEVOTIONAL STUDY

GRACE FOX

AspirePress

Names of God
Living Unafraid: Devotional Study

Copyright © 2024 by Grace Fox
Published by Aspire Press
An imprint of Tyndale House Ministries
Carol Stream, Illinois
www.hendricksonrose.com

ISBN: 978-1-4964-8641-7

Cover and interior design by Cristalle Kishi

Images used under license from Shutterstock.com

Printed in the United States of America
010124VP

Contents

A Note from Grace

Our world is a scary place. Mass shootings claim the innocent. Threats of nuclear warfare loom. Famines, floods, and fires occur with growing frequency. Deadly viruses spread across the globe, overwhelming us with fear and testing the limits of our medical system. As living costs rise, we gasp at our grocery bill and worry about paying the rent or mortgage.

Then there's the moral decline. Christian leaders are being exposed for having private lives that run contrary to their public message. Influencers deconstruct their faith and take their followers with them. Society boasts of behaviors beyond the scope of imagination. Where will the pell-mell race down this path end?

Scary stuff sneaks into our private space too: broken relationships; loneliness; generational strongholds; domestic violence; mental and physical health issues, including the Big C—Cancer. As I write this, five dear friends—all younger than me—are battling advanced stages of the dreaded disease, and other issues I mentioned have hit close to home.

Our minds naturally gravitate toward the negative. The enemy of our souls hoots for joy when we go down that path, because he knows the dangers lurking there. Focusing on the mess and pain can paralyze us with fear, but we don't have to succumb. God wants us to live courageously and freely, and one way we can do so is by anchoring ourselves in the truth of who God is.

Doing so releases us from our perceived need to control our circumstances. It frees us from the habit of hovering over our kids and grandkids. It gives us faith to believe that God will provide when unexpected expenses leave a shortfall. It gives us confidence to say yes when God nudges us to do something for which we feel inadequate.

One way that God helps us focus on the truth about his nature is by revealing his various names in Scripture. Names—especially nicknames—reveal much about their bearer. Remember *Snow White and the Seven Dwarfs*? We understand the dwarfs' personalities by their names: Doc, Grumpy, Happy, Sleepy, Bashful, Sneezy, and Dopey.

When I was a child, my dad dubbed me "Chipper" while on a family vacation in the Rocky Mountains. The inspiration came as he watched a chipmunk dash from one tree trunk to another. He likened the critter's happy, nonstop activity to mine as I played in the woods that day. Dad nailed it: I loved happy, nonstop activity throughout my childhood, and I still thrive on it today.

Likewise, God's names describe who he is. The more we understand the meaning of each of his names, the more we're able to trust him when we face frightening situations. As the psalmist David wrote, "Those who know your name trust in you, for you, O LORD, do not abandon those who search for you" (Psalm 9:10).

I want to be that woman who doesn't waste emotional energy worrying about the worst possible outcome. No matter what comes my way, I want to experience God's peace, which surpasses human understanding (Philippians 4:7). I want to reflect courage and offer hope to those who are without it.

I suspect you share my heart's desire, so let's link arms and take a deep dive into God's names. Together let's discover more about who he is and learn to apply these truths so we can live unafraid.

On a practical note, be aware that I have used common English spellings of the Hebrew names of God, but alternative spellings also exist due to pronunciation differences.

Reading this book on your own is an option, but you may benefit more by using it with a small group or a book club or by inviting a friend to study with you one-on-one. I recommend reading one session per sitting and then completing the study questions. When you meet with your group, share an aha moment you experienced while reading the session, and then learn from one another's insights as you share answers to the questions. Each session also ends with a prayer you can speak aloud so that its life-giving words penetrate your soul. Then expect God to answer.

Writing *Living Unafraid* has grown my faith. My prayer is that yours will blossom as well. I'd love to hear from you when you have a moment to share how this book has impacted your life. Please recommend it to your friends, family, and church ministry leaders. Talk about it on social media, and include a selfie with the book in hand. Post an Amazon review to help others learn about it so they can benefit too. Together let's spark a revival and turn the world upside down for Jesus.

Know you are loved,

Grace

gracefox.com
grace@gracefox.com

PS: Be sure to enjoy the other resources I offer:

- Receive free gifts when you subscribe to my blog and monthly update at gracefox.com/blog.
- Find spiritual encouragement and engage with my Facebook community at fb.com/gracefox.author.
- Follow me on Instagram at instagram.com/graceloewenfox.

Scan the QR code or go to

hendricksonrose.org/LivingUnafraid

to enjoy an introductory video from author Grace Fox.

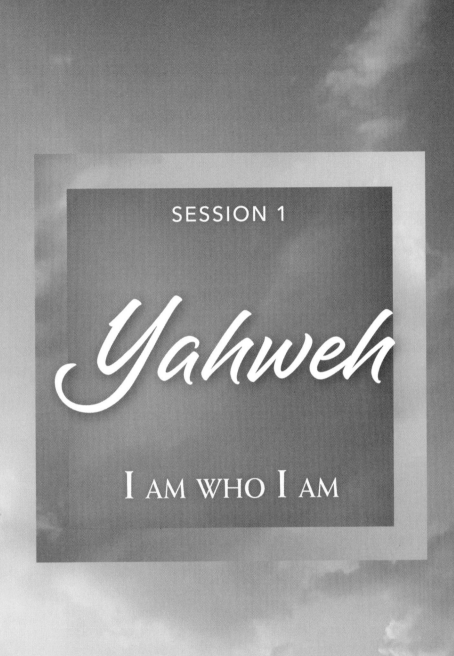

SESSION 1

Yahweh

I am who I am

THE PHONE RANG at eight o'clock one Sunday morning in January 2007. "Do you still sense a change coming in your future?" asked a familiar voice. "If you are, then I think I have something for you."

The caller was one of our former pastors. A couple years earlier, my husband, Gene, and I had told him about a restlessness in our hearts. We were praying and waiting for direction when it seemed God was prying us from the Christian camp where we'd worked for more than a decade.

Our pastor-friend went on to tell us about International Messengers, a global missionary sending and partnering agency. "They're looking for someone to launch a Canadian office," he said. "May I give them your name?"

"Sure. Why not?" Gene replied.

The organization's president called to chat two days later. The rest, as they say, is history. We remained at the camp on Quadra Island, British Columbia, through the busy spring and summer seasons and transitioned to International Messengers near the end of August.

Making the shift involved a massive learning curve, but it also meant finding a home three hours and two ferries away, near Vancouver, British Columbia—one of the world's most expensive places to live. We literally had only a few hours available in late July to locate a house, and we knew our options were limited, so we crunched numbers in our budget and prayed for a miracle.

Only six days after the move, our new ministry would begin with a trip to Slovakia for our first staff conference. The thought of packing our household, moving, unpacking, and making an international trip all within days felt overwhelming, so I added a postscript to our prayer: "God, please give us a clean house that needs no repairs. We have no time for such things." And then I added a second postscript: "Please send someone to care for our cat while we're away."

Did God provide a home within our budget? Yes. He even provided a down payment through an unexpected lump-sum pension payment from the camp.

Did he provide a clean home that needed no repairs? Yes. The owners had painted the walls and laid new carpet in preparation for listing it with a realtor. They also cleaned thoroughly before moving out. It sat vacant and spotless, waiting for new owners to take up residence.

Did he provide someone to care for our cat? Yes. A week before leaving camp, one of our daughters' friends would be getting married. The newlyweds planned to settle in Vancouver, so I asked if they might like to house-sit and feed Simba for two weeks. The bride-to-be was a cat lover and gave an enthusiastic yes.

God addressed Moses's fears in incredible ways. One of them occurred when he introduced himself as Yahweh.

Evidence of God's involvement in our new assignment exceeded our expectations in other ways too. For instance, our new place didn't have space for my piano, so I tried to sell it but had no success. The only option would have been to temporarily squeeze it into our new living room until we could find a buyer.

When a friend showed up to help us unload, he saw the piano and chuckled as he asked, "Where do you plan to put this?" Gene explained the situation, and our friend replied, "I'll buy it. We've been looking for a piano."

God knew this new ministry and moving assignment was faith-stretching for us, so he came alongside and addressed our fears and concerns with evidence of his presence and power. He knew that doing so would erase any second-guesses about whether we were on the right path when challenges faced us down the road.

Friend, God is not a deity who observes us from a distance. He is an up-close and personal Father who wants to engage with his creation. When we draw near to him, he draws near to us. He leans in and listens to our prayers, and he often answers in ways that leave us amazed.

God showed a similar kindness to Moses after giving him a new and faith-testing assignment. He knew the size and scope of this task intimidated Moses, so he came alongside and addressed Moses's fears in incredible ways. One of them occurred when God introduced himself as *Yahweh*.

Yahweh: What Does It Mean?

In Hebrew, the original language of the Old Testament, the name *Yahweh* (pronounced "YAH-way") means "I AM WHO I AM" (Exodus 3:14) or "I WILL BE WHAT I WILL BE."[1] It is often thought to be related to the verb *havah*, which can mean "to be." In our English Bibles, Yahweh is often translated as "LORD" (capital *L* followed by small capital letters) for a few reasons that we'll discuss in just a bit.

Throughout Genesis 1, God is identified only by the name *Elohim*, which speaks to his creative power and transcendence. But in Genesis chapter 2, when the focus becomes God's relationship with his creation, the name *Yahweh* begins to show up, which speaks to his personal and moral nature. It signifies nearness to his creation, and later in the Bible it relates specifically to his chosen people, the Israelites.

When the name *Yahweh* first appears, it is used in combination with *Elohim*: "This is the account of the heavens and the earth when they were created, when the LORD [*Yahweh*] God [*Elohim*] made the earth and the heavens" (Genesis 2:4 NIV). Used together, the names *Yahweh* (LORD) and *Elohim* (God) tell us that the God who created heaven and earth and the God who made an everlasting covenant of love with Israel is one and the same.

The name *Yahweh* appears throughout the rest of Genesis, but it is not until Exodus 3 that we get an explanation of this name. In verse 4, God calls to Moses from a burning bush and commands him to lead the enslaved Israelites out of Egypt. After Moses expresses his fears about doing this, God uses the name *Yahweh* to introduce himself, which he prefaces with an "I AM" description:

> Moses said to God, "Suppose I go to the Israelites and say to them, 'The God of your fathers has sent me to you,' and they ask me, 'What is his name?' Then what shall I tell them?"
>
> God said to Moses, "I AM WHO I AM. This is what you are to say to the Israelites: 'I AM has sent me to you.'"
>
> God also said to Moses, "Say to the Israelites, 'The LORD [Yahweh], the God of your fathers—the God of Abraham, the God of Isaac and the God of Jacob—has sent me to you.'
>
> "This is my name forever,
>   the name you shall call me
>   from generation to generation."

EXODUS 3:13–15 NIV

In our North American culture and in many other cultures around the world, people often introduce themselves with the customary greeting, "Hi. My name is _____." Depending on the person and the circumstances surrounding our meeting, I might say, "My name is Grace" or "My name is Grace Fox." I might even say, "My name is Mrs. Fox." We state the name by which we prefer to be known by that person.

God did the same when he used the name *Yahweh* to introduce himself to Moses. As the king over heaven and earth, he could have used a formal title such as "Your Majesty." As judge, he could have used the title "Your Honor." As our heavenly Father, he could have introduced himself as "Abba." But he did not. The name by which he chose to be known was *Yahweh*, so what was he communicating?

First, we've already noted that *Yahweh* could mean "I AM WHO I AM" or "I WILL BE WHAT I WILL BE." Based on these interpretations, the name declares that God is not a nebulous force floating through time and space. He's not a collection of cosmic energies emitting positive vibes. Rather, he's a person. He's real. He's alive. And he wants connection with his creation. By using the name *Yahweh*, God described himself to Moses as a God who desires to be close to his people.

Second, this name reveals that God is self-existent. That is, nothing contributes to his existence. We can't say the same about ourselves: My mother gave birth to me, and I gave birth to three children. Minus their dad and me, they would never have come into being.

Or consider that we depend on oxygen, water, and food to keep us alive. We take medicine to treat our illnesses. We seek wise counsel when we have a problem. But God depends on nothing to sustain himself; he's *the source* of everything on which all living things depend. *Yahweh is* because he is God (John 5:26).

Third, God's self-existence makes him eternal. The sun might forget to shine, the rains fail to fall, and plants cease to grow, but none of these circumstances would affect him. The heavens and earth will pass away (Matthew 24:35), but God remains forever because he relies on nothing for his existence. Everything created is temporal, but he was not created; therefore, he is not temporal. *Yahweh* is forever because he is God (Psalm 102:27).

Fourth, God never changes. Pastor Tony Evans writes,

> We are forever changing. We're getting older, our hair is graying, we're getting wrinkles, and our skin is sagging. Our memories aren't always what they used to be. But God doesn't go through that process. He is who He was, and He is also who He will be because the great I Am never steps out of the present tense. In other words, He is always *now*.[2]

Cultural norms, laws, governments, fashion, family structures, weather and traffic patterns, the cost of living, modes of transportation—all of these change over time, and so do we. But *Yahweh* remains the same.

He is relevant yesterday, today, and tomorrow, because he is God (Hebrews 13:8).

Finally, God is who he is. He didn't go to school to learn his creative skills. No one taught or mentored him. Circumstances didn't shape or refine him. He is who he is because he is God. It's vital to remember that God is not what we try to make him to be. He far exceeds the scope of our wildest imagination. He's holier than our minds can fathom. He is bigger, stronger, wiser, more compassionate, and more faithful than we can pretend to understand.

The truth God communicated about himself through the name *Yahweh* has not changed. He thought it was important for Moses to know way back then, and we can be sure it's no less important for us now. Let's take a closer look at what Moses learned.

Moses Discovers God as *Yahweh*

Leading the Israelites out of captivity in Egypt was a God-sized task, and Moses felt far from capable. He wondered why God had chosen him, of all people.

Moses had just spent forty years tending his father-in-law's flocks. Forty years hiding from Pharaoh, regretting his murderous reaction when he saw an Egyptian bully beat up an Israelite. Surely God had confused him with someone else. This was a case of mistaken identity, right?

Wrong. God had made Moses for this moment in time; and knowing the enormity of the task, God promised his presence to guide, provide, and protect.

From Moses's perspective, however, the promise offered little consolation, because he'd never experienced God up close and personal. His understanding of God was limited to *Elohim*—the powerful, genius Creator whom Moses may have thought remained distant from his creation.

YAHWEH 101

- In Jewish tradition, God's name is considered too sacred to speak. Ancient Jewish scribes would not read the name aloud and at some point stopped using the name directly in Hebrew writing. According to some, Jewish priests would not say God's name either, except once a year on the Day of Atonement, in the inner sanctuary of the Temple. As a result, the actual pronunciation has been lost, although some scholars believe it may have been pronounced "YAH-weh"

- The ancient Hebrew language did not use vowels, so *Yahweh* is made up of only four consonants: *yod* (י), *he* (ה) (pronounced "hay"), *vav* (ו), and *he* (ה). In English, this name is represented by the letters *Y-H-V-H* or *Y-H-W-H* (the latter since it has often been thought that *vav* was pronounced with a *w* sound in ancient Hebrew).

- When vowel markings were finally added to the Hebrew Bible more than a thousand years ago, vowels from the word *Adonai*, which means "my Lord," were added to YHWH. When reading Scripture, this served as a reminder to substitute *Adonai*, since it was not acceptable to pronounce God's personal name.

- When this consonant and vowel combination was first translated into English hundreds of years ago, it was sometimes written as "Jehovah" since *Y* becomes *J* in some languages. But this isn't an accurate representation of God's name, since the vowel markings were for an altogether different word (*Adonai*).

- Appearing more than six thousand times in the Old Testament, *Yahweh*'s usage far exceeds any other name or title for God. One thing is certain: God wants us to know that his intent has always been to have a relationship with us.

Besides, Moses's direct interaction with God at the burning bush didn't exactly leave him with warm, fuzzy feelings. "'Do not come any closer' [God] said. 'Take off your sandals, for the place where you are standing is holy ground.... I am the God [*Elohim*] of your father, the God of Abraham, the God of Isaac and the God of Jacob'" (Exodus 3:5–6 NIV). After this, Moses hid his face because he was afraid to look at God. His fear escalated when God told him to confront Pharaoh and lead the Israelites out of captivity.

Then God introduced himself as *Yahweh*, the God of Moses's ancestors, and began to interact with Moses on a new level. He offered verbal assurances and visual proof of his presence and power: First he turned Moses's staff into a snake and back into a staff (Exodus 4:2–4). Next he made Moses's hand leprous and restored it to health (verses 6–7). Then he reminded Moses that he had made his mouth and would empower him to speak (verses 11–12).

But fear had taken a foothold, and Moses resisted. "Pardon your servant, Lord," he said. "Please send someone else" (Exodus 4:13 NIV). Did you catch how Moses addressed *Yahweh*? He called him "Lord." When *Lord* is used in the Old Testament (capital "L" with lowercase "ord"), it's usually a direct translation of the Hebrew word *Adonai*—the name of God that denotes his lordship and authority. This is different from "LORD," which we've already learned is how God's personal name, YHWH (*Yahweh*), is often translated.

It's possible that Moses used the name *Adonai* because *Yahweh* was too sacred to speak. But do you see the contradiction? Moses addressed God using the name that emphasizes God's lordship, and in the same breath, he denied his lordship by declining to do what God was calling him to. Why would Moses do such a thing?

I suspect that deep down inside, he had developed an inaccurate understanding of God's character. Wrong thinking resulted in fear, and fear led to disobedience. We might be tempted to tsk-tsk him, but we do the same thing:

- God nudges us to donate to a ministry organization or a family in crisis, but an inaccurate understanding of his ability to provide results in our fear that we won't have enough to care for our own needs. This leads to our withholding funds.

- God prompts us to go on a short-term missions trip or teach a Bible study or become a foster parent, but an inaccurate understanding of his power to equip us for the role results in our fear of inadequacy. Therefore, we decline the opportunity.

- God prods us to share words of encouragement with a stranger who is obviously distraught, but an inaccurate understanding of the depths of his compassion means we fear being misunderstood as nosy. This leads to our silence.

Fear is natural when God gives us an assignment, but our response reveals what we believe to be true about him. We can let fear paralyze us, or we can see it as the portal through which we experience God in new ways. Thankfully, Moses stepped through the portal, and sure enough, he experienced God as *Yahweh* in mind-boggling ways.

For starters, *Yahweh* struck the Egyptians with ten plagues as part of his rescue mission (Exodus 7:14–11:10). That was history in the making, but *Yahweh* did so much more for both Moses as an individual and the entire nation of Israel. Here are a few highlights:

- He led the Israelites through the wilderness in a cloud by day and a pillar of fire by night (Exodus 13:21).

- He split the Red Sea so the Israelites could escape from the Egyptian army (Exodus 14:21–31).

- He provided the Israelites with drinking water and manna in the wilderness (Exodus 15:25; 16:4; 17:5-6).

- He invited Moses to meet him on Mount Sinai. The glory of God descended in a cloud upon the mountain, and Moses entered that cloud and remained on the mountain for forty days (Exodus 24:15–18).

- During that time on Mount Sinai, God gave Moses the covenant of his laws and instructions for building the tabernacle so that he could dwell with his people (Exodus 25:1–31:18).

- In the tent of meeting, God spoke with Moses as with a friend (Exodus 33:7–11).

- God personally buried Moses when he died (Deuteronomy 34:5–6).

Moses was afraid of God when he stood at the burning bush, but eventually, his fear turned to friendship. Seeing *Yahweh* in action on his behalf and spending time in *Yahweh*'s presence aligned Moses's beliefs with truth; and Moses, once a herdsman in hiding, became a heralded hero of the Bible.

Perhaps you feel afraid too. Maybe God has given you an assignment that makes you want to say, "Please, Lord, find someone else." If so, I want you to pause for a few minutes to ask yourself the following questions:

1. What is God asking me to do?
2. What fear is holding me back?
3. What inaccurate beliefs about God lie at the root of my fear?

When you've answered those questions, ask God to align your thoughts about him with the truth—and to give you the faith and courage to say yes to him no matter what he asks.

Rita's Story: Choosing to Trust

The name *Yahweh*—"I am who I am"—gives us courage not only to accept God-given assignments but also to navigate suffering. Rita Schulte is a professional counselor who suffered several losses over a short span of time. In her book *Shattered*, she writes,

The bottom drops out, and people offer trite clichés about trusting God and surrendering ourselves to his will. If only it were that easy. But humans equate God's goodness with how we want our stories to play out. If things turn out well, it's easy to trust God. If they don't, we have nowhere to build a foundation of trust.[3]

Rita's story did not play out the way she wanted. Her difficult season began when she suffered the loss of her mom, with whom she'd been very close. Then she witnessed lightning strike her teenage son and daughter as they parasailed while vacationing in Florida. She watched helplessly as the pair fell twenty stories into the ocean. They survived only because the boat driver and his coworker miraculously resuscitated them.

A couple of years after that trauma, Rita's dad was diagnosed with metastatic bone cancer, and Rita cared for him in her home as his health declined. She adored him, but the responsibility and isolation involved with round-the-clock caregiving taxed her. Watching him slip away broke her heart and revived all the emotions she'd experienced during the other painful events. *Everyone I love will be taken from me*, she thought. *Everything about which I'm certain will change.*

Anxiety, depression, and panic attacks set in. She lost her appetite and ability to sleep. Some days she lay curled in a ball or stared blankly into space. "I landed in a dark place because I hadn't paid attention to what was happening in my heart as losses piled up," Rita told me. "But while I was finding it difficult to trust God, he began using my suffering to teach me about his nature and character through the name I AM. It showed up everywhere I looked. God whispered it to me over and over so I could find him in the dark abyss of grief."

At first, Rita noticed that well-wishers' greeting cards all contained messages with the name I AM. Then a friend sent her two teaching tapes that addressed fear and I AM's presence in the places of suffering. As she listened, she thumbed through an old notebook and discovered a piece of paper with "I AM THAT I AM" written in bold, red print. She'd placed it there four years earlier when she was scouring Scripture for answers to why God had spared her children's lives but allowed a friend's daughter to take her own life. Finding that slip of paper four years later was not coincidental.

After one particularly rough day of nonstop panic attacks, Rita was searching for something to calm herself and randomly pulled an audiotape from a massive collection in her closet. It featured Bible teacher Kay Arthur speaking about the time when Jesus's disciples encountered a storm while sailing to Capernaum: "A gale swept down upon them, and the sea grew very rough. They had rowed three or four miles when suddenly they saw Jesus walking on the water toward the boat. They were terrified, but he called out to them, 'Don't be afraid. I am here!'" (John 6:18–20).

> Yahweh *wants you to know and experience him as the all-sufficient, everything-you-will-ever-need God.*

Something powerful stirred in Rita's soul as Kay explained that Jesus's declaration of "I am" mirrored God's "I AM" statement to Moses. That's when she realized God wasn't just whispering his name to her; he was shouting it. "Do not be afraid! *I am! I am* the all-sufficient, all-you-will-ever-need God." Fear lost its grip as she chose to believe that God held her securely in his grip.

"That day, I caught a glimpse of God's heart when he saw that mine was breaking, and I knew I could trust him. He cared enough to show up in ways that were beyond reason," said Rita. "The losses God allowed challenged my nice, neat theology and my formula for making life work. I had to choose between feeling angry and bitter or trusting in God. Thankfully, I chose trust—not because I'm a great Christian, but because God worked in my heart."

Experiencing *Yahweh*'s presence matured Rita's faith and prepared her for the profound loss of her husband and soulmate to suicide, three years after her dad died. Again, *Yahweh* showed up consistently, this time as Aslan, the lion featured so prominently in C. S. Lewis's Chronicles of Narnia series. Everywhere Rita turned, the lion appeared in pictures, stuffies, and ornaments, as though to reassure her that she was not alone. She knew beyond a doubt that I AM—the all-sufficient, everything-you-will-ever-need God—was with her and would protect, guide, and strengthen her in this new and unexpected journey.

Rita's path is not one she would have chosen, but by facing the fear of losing her loved ones, she entered the portal through which she discovered God in a deeper, sweeter, richer way. Catching a glimpse of *Yahweh*'s love and engagement in her life freed her from fear and enabled her to trust him.

Perhaps you've suffered too. Maybe you're in that hard place right now. Oh, my friend, I wish I could promise that everything's going to be fine and your story will turn out as you wish. I can't make such a promise, because I don't know God's plans for your life. But of this one thing I am sure: *Yahweh* wants you to know and experience him as the all-sufficient, everything-you-will-ever-need God, especially in the hard places of life.

Jesus's Claim to the Name

When God stated to Moses that his name was *Yahweh*, he was making the supreme declaration, "I AM WHO I AM." Jesus echoed this while teaching in the temple in Jerusalem. His audience identified themselves as Abraham's children, but some had an attitude toward him that proved otherwise. Unlike Abraham, who had looked forward to Jesus's coming, they refused to believe that Jesus was the promised Messiah. They demanded,

> *"You aren't even fifty years old. How can you say you have seen Abraham?"*
>
> *Jesus answered, "I tell you the truth, before Abraham was even born, I AM!"*

JOHN 8:57–58

By using the phrase "I AM," Jesus stated that he existed before Abraham and thus equated himself with God. This was considered blasphemy and infuriated his listeners: "At that point they picked up stones to throw at him. But Jesus was hidden from them and left the Temple" (John 8:59).

Jesus made the same declaration on the night he was arrested in the garden of Gethsemane. When the temple guards and Roman troops showed up with lanterns, torches, and weapons, he asked a leading question: "Who are you looking for?" They replied, "Jesus the Nazarene." "'I AM he,' Jesus said" (John 18:4–5).

Every Jewish person within earshot recognized "I AM" as the same phrase God used when he introduced himself to Moses. Hearing it bore a profound impact, for John 18:6 says that "as Jesus said 'I AM he,' they all drew back and fell to the ground!"

Imagine this entire crowd keeling over backward at the sound of "I AM he"! Even the Roman soldiers felt the strong impact of God's name spoken by Christ, God in the flesh (Colossians 2:9). Such is the unleashed power of God's name.

For as long as I can remember, I've heard prayers end with "In Jesus's name." I'm guilty of parroting the phrase without stopping to think about what it means. I admit falling into rote mode, where "In Jesus's name" becomes an automatic conclusion to my conversation with God. A tidy little bow in which to wrap my prayer requests.

But no more.

Studying the names of God has turned my prayer life upside down. I realize now that praying in the authority of Jesus's name carries the power to flatten our enemies. No force can stand against it. Fear releases its grip and falls to the ground at the mere mention of the name I AM.

The book of John contains several other instances where Jesus made definitive "I AM" statements. Each one points to the truth that he is the all-sufficient, all-you-will-ever-need God:

- To all who hunger for spiritual truth, he says, "I am the bread of life" (John 6:35).

- To all who fumble in the darkness, he says, "I am the light of the world" (John 8:12).

- To all who seek shelter for their soul, he says, "I am the gate for the sheep" (John 10:7).

- To all who long to belong, he says, "I am the good shepherd" (John 10:11).

- To all who crave abundant and eternal life, he says, "I am the resurrection and the life" (John 11:25).

- To all who pursue the path to God, he says, "I am the way, the truth, and the life" (John 14:6).

- To all who desire a fruitful life, he says, "I am the true grapevine" (John 15:1).

What is your deepest need today? Go ahead—tell Jesus about it. You don't have to use fancy words or spiritual-sounding language, because he already knows what it is. Be honest with him about your hopes and fears. Pour out your heart and pray with faith in Jesus's name. Trust him to unleash his power on your behalf.

How Shall We Respond?

God revealed his name *Yahweh* to show that he wants us to know him and experience his involvement in our lives moment by moment. This purpose diametrically opposes Satan's plans to destroy us, so Satan, the enemy of our souls, unleashes his fury upon everything the name *Yahweh* represents.

Adam and Eve enjoyed friendship with God until the day the serpent (Satan) slithered onto the scene and asked Eve, "Did God really say you must not eat the fruit from any of the trees in the garden?" (Genesis 3:1).

I'd heard the garden of Eden story my entire life but only recently discovered Satan's strategy hidden in this verse. The clue lies in how he phrased the question he asked Eve.

As we've already seen, beginning in Genesis 2:4, the name of God used in the creation story is "LORD God"—the combination of *Yahweh*, which represents the personal aspect of God, and *Elohim*, which is less personal. When speaking to Eve, Satan used only the name "God"—he did not include "LORD" (*Yahweh*), thereby minimizing the possibility that Eve would think about the relational side of God. We see it in her response: "It's only the fruit from the tree in the middle of the garden that we are not allowed to eat. *God* said, 'You must not eat it or even touch it; if you do, you will die'" (Genesis 3:3, emphasis added).

Bingo! Mission accomplished. Eve succumbed to temptation the moment she minimized—or worse, negated—her relationship with *Yahweh*. According to Tony Evans,

> When [*Yahweh*] is brought into the conversation, God is a personal, interactive being who made, purposed, designed, and intimately knows both Adam and Eve. Satan was okay with Eve acknowledging God; he just didn't want her having a personal relationship under [*Yahweh*'s] authority.[4]

Satan is devious but not very smart. He has used the same strategy throughout the ages, and his tactics remain the same today. He doesn't care whether we believe *Elohim* exists—"even the demons believe this, and they tremble in terror" (James 2:19). It's our relationship with *Yahweh* that unnerves him, so he focuses his efforts there.

Satan's usual methods involve planting in our minds doubts or outright lies about God's character. Doubts and lies lead to mistrust, and mistrust leads to fear. Fear stops us from saying yes to God when he invites us to join him in a faith-stretching assignment. It hinders us from trusting him in the face of an uncertain future, and it hinders us from trusting him for our loved ones' well-being. We lose sleep, worry about the what-ifs, and slip into control mode. Fear persuades us that God needs our help, so we take matters into our own hands and rush ahead of him or take a path contrary to the one he wants for us.

If we don't fall for the lies, then Satan tries another tactic to minimize our relationship with *Yahweh*: busyness. Often from fear of saying no, we say yes too many times and end up rushing from one commitment to the next. What we're doing might be good, but spending time with *Yahweh* gets relegated to the back burner.

Lies. Busyness. And a third tactic: voices. We live in an age inundated with voices telling us what to believe—voices that especially like to prey on our fears. Some speak from a place of deep personal pain that has never been addressed; some speak from a self-centered belief system; others speak from suspicion about the society in which we live and the leaders who make decisions about the direction it goes. To which voices do we listen and turn for advice?

Let's exercise caution here and tune our ears to the Holy Spirit's whispers rather than the myriad voices vying for our attention. Satan is okay with our playing church and dipping our big toes into religion, but he's not okay with our decision to get serious with *Yahweh*. Going deeper with him unravels Satan's devious plans and threatens to derail his destructive purposes.

Let's join hands and take a stand. Together let's become that threat. Let's choose this day to make *Yahweh* our first love and to live fearlessly according to his directives. This begins by making a habit of spending time in his presence, as Moses did when he entered the tent to meet with God (Exodus 33:9–11).

You can pitch your own tent too: Find a regular place to meet with *Yahweh*, if only for a few minutes each day. Keep a basket handy with your Bible, pen, and journal so you don't waste time hunting for them. Ask the Holy Spirit to quiet your heart so you can hear his voice, and expect him to speak to you through Scripture. Follow a Bible reading plan to stay on track, unless you've developed a plan that works for you.

Setting aside a chunk of time alone with God was difficult when my kids were toddlers. I rose early with good intentions, but the children always woke up a minute or two later. Coordinating everyone's afternoon naptime helped me establish a routine that allowed a few minutes to read the Word and pray. Sometimes my brain was too tired to absorb more than a few verses, but I learned to be okay with that. My prayer was always, "God, give me one new insight about yourself today," and he did.

Early mornings worked best as the kids grew older. One day as I was trying to reestablish a routine, I asked God to wake me at the time he wanted to meet. He impressed five o'clock on my mind. I thought he was kidding, so I asked him to wake me up without an alarm at the time of his choosing. He consistently did so—at five o'clock. Envisioning him waiting for me in the living room took the sting out of rising before dawn.

Now an empty nester, I'm in a season where I rise earlier than five o'clock to spend time with *Yahweh*. It sets the focus and tone for my entire day. It's a joy, not a hardship. Life seasons change, and the specifics of our personal time with God changes with them. Be flexible and find what works best for you.

Moses's life suggests another action we can take to get serious about our relationship with *Yahweh*. That is, we can *ask* to know him more intimately. When *Yahweh* reassured Moses that he knew Moses by name, Moses replied, "Then show me your glorious presence" (Exodus 33:18). We may have to change a few things in our lives to see that prayer answered. For example, we may need to replace much of the time we spend on Netflix or social media with Bible teaching or Christian podcasts. We may also need to retrain our brains from entertaining negative or impure thoughts to focusing on God's truth (Romans 12:2).

When we ask God to give us an insatiable desire for him and his Word, he will say yes. *Yahweh* will come alongside, show us where to make necessary changes to align our hearts and minds with truth, and then help us to make those changes. As Pastor Michael Gowens states, "Whatever the problem you face, he is the solution. Whatever your need, he can fill it. Whatever your circumstance, he can change it."[5] *Yahweh*—"I AM WHO I AM"—loves you and wants a close relationship with you. What an amazing privilege! Call on his great name today, my friend.

Prayer

Yahweh, I praise you for being the great I AM–my self-sufficient, all-sufficient God. Thank you for being up close and personal with me, for drawing near to your children and satisfying every need. I acknowledge you as my sole source of wisdom, strength, and courage. I face no challenge too big or temptation too strong when my heart is aligned with yours. Help me walk in the truth of this manifestation of your character, and transform me through the process. In Jesus's name, amen.

Points TO *Ponder*

1 **Read Psalm 139:1–5.**

■ How does this passage demonstrate God's personal interest in our lives, represented by his name *Yahweh*?

■ What part of this psalm resonates most with you, and why?

2 **Read Jeremiah 10:6 and compare it with John 18:4–6.**

■ What's your takeaway on the topic of praying in Jesus's name?

■ How will it affect the mindset with which you approach prayer, especially in times of fear?

3 **Read Psalm 89:15–16.**

  ■ What difference does being mindful of God's presence make in your day-to-day life?

  ■ How about during times of turmoil?

  ■ How about when you're facing temptation?

4 **Read Psalm 113:1–3.**

  ■ What command is given regarding the name *Yahweh*?

  ■ Jot down at least three things for which you can give praise to our all-sufficient God.

  ■ Pause here and express your praise to him.

5

Review the "I AM" statements listed under the heading "Jesus's Claim to the Name."

- Now consider the current state of your heart and fill in this blank: "I am _____." (For example, "fearful," "spiritually malnourished," "lonely," "seeking for truth," etc.)

- How can Jesus fill your need?

- Invite him to do so.

Scan the QR code or go to

hendricksonrose.org/ LivingUnafraidSession1

for more author insights about the name *Yahweh*.

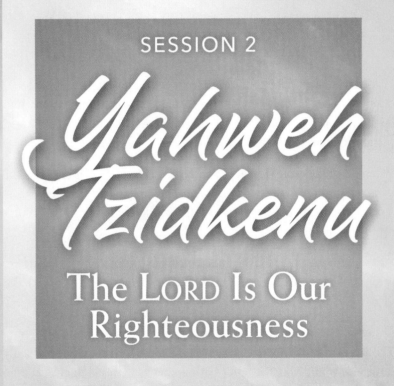

SESSION 2

Yahweh Tzidkenu

The Lord Is Our Righteousness

I GREW UP in an environment that synced righteousness with religious rules.

For instance, no one in my circle used a regular card deck because the king, queen, and jack were considered sinful. Dancing was also taboo. I was in fourth grade when my parents asked that I be excused from gym class because square dancing was part of the curriculum. When my classmates asked why I didn't join the fun, I answered, "Square dancing is against my religion." That's all I knew to say.

Movies were forbidden too. I was a sixth grader when a friend who was celebrating her birthday invited me to a kids' matinee and then back to her home for cake. Knowing my folks would nix the matinee, I neglected to mention that part to them.

When Saturday came, I lined up with the other partygoers outside the theatre, waiting for the doors to open. The building was located on the block-long main street—and wouldn't you know it? Mom chose that time to shop downtown.

Yes, she saw me. And yes, she pulled me from the line. She let me attend the rest of the party, but again I answered my friends' curiosity with the same basic line: "Going to movies is against my religion."

Always the testy middle child, I asked what made theaters off-limits. The answer? "You wouldn't want Jesus to find you there if he suddenly returned, would you?" I didn't have a clue what Jesus might do if he caught me watching a Mickey Mouse flick in a God-forbidden place, but the thought scared the willies out of me.

Fortunately, my childhood positives outweighed the negatives, and I graduated from high school intent on becoming a missionary. A Bible college with a reputation for training missionaries accepted my application, so off I went.

The religious rules I'd already learned were few compared to the regulations this school instituted to encourage spiritual maturity. For example, contemporary worship music was banned because the beat was considered worldly. The same label applied to makeup and pierced ears.

On registration day, the dean of women politely informed me that my hair was too short because my stylish cut failed to cover the top of my ears. Strike one.

One afternoon, my dorm resident assistant knocked on my door. "Grace, I don't think your skirt meets the regulations," she said. "Would you please kneel so I can measure it?" The hem landed about a half inch above the floor. Strike two.

Cultivating opposite-sex friendships during our freshman and sophomore years was also a no-go. Relationships were allowed for juniors and seniors, but only with the dean of students' permission and stringent guidelines.

I recall standing in the center of campus my senior year, chatting for a couple of minutes with a male classmate on the day Christmas break began. A teacher saw us from his second-story office window and came outside to tell us to move along. Strike three.

With due respect, the school did help me form beneficial spiritual disciplines, but some of the rules bred more hypocrisy than holiness. I complied on the outside but defied on the inside.

Two years after graduation, I met Gene. We connected instantly while volunteering at a Christian camp, and he proposed by summer's end. My heart pounded when I phoned my folks to tell them about this man who shared my passion for international missions and wanted to marry me.

As I suspected might happen, one of their first comments focused on Gene's last name. "Fox. That's not Mennonite." My maiden name was Loewen, and they'd always assumed I'd find a man from the Mennonite tradition—a Thiessen or Klassen; a Bergen or Barg; a Schellenberg, Schmidt, Froese, or Funk. Anything but a Fox. After all, how could someone bearing a blatant non-Mennonite name be a good Christian?

Then came the question, "Does he play cards?" My answer didn't go well, considering their conviction that playing cards was the devil's tool. Professing Christians who enjoyed this pastime were obviously backslidden.

I assured my parents that I hadn't sold my soul to the devil. Rather, I'd given my heart to a man who loved Jesus. "And he's a good man, even if his name isn't Mennonite and he enjoys playing cards," I said.

God understands our inability to achieve righteousness, so he took care of the problem.

(I'll tell you the rest of the story later, I promise. I can laugh about it now, but it wasn't funny then.)

Based on my upbringing, though, Gene came with two strikes already against him. Two became three when, a few days before our wedding, my dad heard him say "Darn." He was given a tongue-lashing and made to promise he would never say it again.

My oh my. It's ludicrous to think that we flawed human beings can make ourselves holy and acceptable in God's eyes by following the rules we create or by bearing the right name. Sometimes I wonder how my soul survived the religious rule-book ride.

We mean well, but our good intentions tangle us in knots. Rather than becoming holy, we become holier-than-thou without recognizing that our attitudes and behaviors are rooted in the fear of disappointing God—a fear that results from an inaccurate understanding of who he is.

But here's the good news: God knows our human nature better than we do and understands our inability to achieve righteousness no matter how hard we try, so he took care of the problem. That's what the name *Yahweh Tzidkenu* is all about, and I can hardly wait to explore it with you.

Yahweh Tzidkenu: What Does It Mean?

The word *Tzidkenu* (pronounced "tzeed-KAY-noo") comes from the Hebrew word *tzedek*, which translates as "justice, rightness, righteousness."[1] *Tzedek* is found more than a hundred times in the Old Testament, but only twice as part of this compound name, which means "The LORD Is Our Righteousness." Both instances are in the book of Jeremiah:

> *"The time is coming,"*
> *says the LORD,*
> *"when I will raise up a righteous descendant*
> *from King David's line.*
> *He will be a King who rules with wisdom.*
> *He will do what is just and right throughout the land.*
> *And this will be his name:*
> *'The LORD Is Our Righteousness'* [*Yahweh Tzidkenu*].
> *In that day Judah will be saved,*
> *and Israel will live in safety."*

JEREMIAH 23:5–6

> *In that day Judah will be saved,*
> *and Jerusalem will live in safety.*
> *And this will be its name:*
> *"The LORD Is Our Righteousness."*

JEREMIAH 33:16

The second usage applies this name to Jerusalem. At the time Jeremiah wrote these words, the ten northern tribes of Israel were living in captivity because they had rebelled against God. Judah, the Southern Kingdom, was spiraling into idolatry and immorality. Having failed to learn a lesson from the Northern Kingdom's plight, the people in the South hardened their hearts toward God and descended deeper into the evil practices of the nations around them.

It was a dark time in Israel's history. The spiritual climate appeared hopeless, but it would not remain so forever. *Yahweh*, who desires to be close to his people, promised to forgive them if they turned back to him. Their beloved Jerusalem would be rebuilt and the temple restored, and they would once again prosper and live in safety.

Best of all, *Yahweh* would give them a new spiritual beginning by *becoming* their righteousness through the descendant Jeremiah mentioned. Theologians agree that this descendant refers to Jesus Christ. He fulfilled this prophecy as a descendant of King David and as the righteous, sinless son of God (Luke 3:21–31). Because we are incapable of righteous living on our own, Jesus came to earth to impart righteousness to all who place their faith in him.

Let's dive deeper into what *righteousness* means and why it matters.

Understanding Righteousness

One online dictionary defines *righteous* as "morally upright; without guilt or sin."[2] Synonyms include words like *upright, just,* and *blameless.* Only God fits these descriptions, of course. Within the context of righteousness, the Bible describes him as unequaled:

- ■ "The Lord is righteous in everything he does; he is filled with kindness." (Psalm 145:17)

- ■ "Everything he does reveals his glory and majesty. His righteousness never fails." (Psalm 111:3)

- ■ "Your righteousness, O God, reaches to the highest heavens. You have done such wonderful things. Who can compare with you, O God?" (Psalm 71:19)

Who can compare with God when it comes to righteousness?

That's a great question. The apostle Paul gave us the answer: "As the Scriptures say, 'No one is righteous—not even one. No one is truly wise; no one is seeking God. All have turned away; all have become useless. No one does good, not a single one'" (Romans 3:10–12). How many times did Paul say "no one"? How many times did he say "all"? If you think he made a bunch of blanket statements, you're correct. So was he.

We pay our taxes, obey the speed limit, leave nice tips when we eat out, and refrain from losing our temper. We attend church, volunteer in the nursery, tithe, and lead small-group studies. We say grace before meals, read our Bibles several times a week, visit shut-ins, remain faithful to our spouse, and give money to the homeless.

All those things are nice, and doing them makes us feel good. But because our hearts are inherently sinful, those actions don't make us righteous or without sin. We pay our taxes but complain about how much the government takes from our paychecks. We hold our temper but hold bitterness too. We read our Bibles because that's what Christians do, not because our souls crave God's Word. We remain faithful to our spouse but entertain lustful thoughts about someone else. And the list goes on.

From the beginning of time, God's plan has been to rescue us from our measly efforts to make ourselves morally blameless, because he knows our endeavors fail. Here's why: "We are all infected and impure with sin. When we display our righteous deeds, they are nothing but filthy rags. Like autumn leaves, we wither and fall, and our sins sweep us away like the wind" (Isaiah 64:6).

Our best efforts to make ourselves morally blameless are as ineffective as the fig leaves Adam and Eve used to cover their nakedness (Genesis 3:7). In his mercy, God exchanged their flimsy, man-made coverings for clothing made from animal skins; but providing this better covering meant shedding blood (verse 21).

In similar fashion, God removes our filthy self-righteous rags and wraps us in his righteousness robe, made possible through the blood of Jesus, shed on the cross:

> *Adam's one sin brings condemnation for everyone, but*
> *Christ's one act of righteousness brings a right relationship*

with God and new life for everyone. Because one person disobeyed God, many became sinners. But because one other person obeyed God, many will be made righteous.

ROMANS 5:18–19

In unspiritual terms, imagine exchanging a dirty, ripped-up bathrobe found in a dumpster for a brand-new designer robe fit for royalty. That's what God has done for us. He has us covered in the righteousness department—literally. What a gift of immeasurable worth!

By manifesting himself through his name *Yahweh Tzidkenu*, God assures us that we don't have to live in the bondage of keeping religious rules to earn his approval. And we don't need to hide from him in fear when we fall short of obeying his commands, as Adam and Eve did.

We can stop striving to be perfect, because none of us are. No amount of rule-keeping or good-works-doing can create blameless hearts or make us righteous people. Only God can do that, and he's masterful at it.

But while some try to make themselves righteous through good works, others think they're so messed up that God can neither forgive nor fix them.

Nothing is further from the truth, my friend, because God's robe of righteousness fits all, and he is also a master at mending broken hearts.

Donna's Story: "I Was Free!"

Donna's heart raced at the sight of the flashing blue lights in her rearview mirror, and for good reason: She was transporting illegal drugs for a dealer with whom she'd had an on-again, off-again relationship for several years.

She had accompanied him on previous runs, but this was the first one on her own. When he'd asked her to do it, she agreed as a means of showing loyalty.

The state highway patrol officer had stopped Donna for an unsafe lane change but then became suspicious of this young woman driving a brand-new, fancy red car in an area notorious for drug trafficking. A search of the vehicle confirmed his suspicions.

Within an hour, Donna was being interrogated by a half dozen FBI agents. They wanted to know the source of the drugs in her possession, but she refused to disclose her friend's name for fear of being labeled a snitch.

A local officer cuffed her wrists and ankles and took her to the police station, where authorities processed her and placed her in a holding cell. She felt humiliated and ashamed. *What have I done to myself?* she thought. *I'm only twenty-one, but my life is over.*

Donna's life had been anything but easy. Raised as a latchkey kid by a single mom in a crime-riddled neighborhood, circumstances forced her to grow up fast. Male relatives began molesting her when she was eight, but she told no one. Despite feeling violated, ashamed, and angry at herself and those who hurt her, she believed this type of trauma was normal for her life.

God's robe of righteousness fits all, and he is also a master at mending broken hearts.

Donna became promiscuous at age fourteen, after her mom began working the night shift. She told herself that she didn't care about what was happening to her, but she was drowning emotionally. Sometimes she sat in a closet and cried for hours. Amazingly, Donna managed to complete high school and then moved away to attend college. That's when she met the man who later convinced her to make the drug run.

"I didn't know my worth," said Donna as she shared her story with me. "I was dealing with rejection and abandonment issues, and I thought I was ugly and tarnished. When this guy noticed me and called me a cutie, I clung to him. I figured that everything would be okay if I could just get him to love me, so I figured I'd be loyal to him no matter what."

Three years later, her loyalty exacted a high cost. After Donna's arrest, a judge considered her a flight risk and set her bond at half a million dollars. Raising that amount was impossible, so she sat in jail for seventeen months before settling on a plea bargain. During that time, inmates were under lockdown for twenty-one hours every day and were not even allowed to watch television.

Donna lost hope. Facing a possible fourteen-year prison sentence drove her to contemplate suicide. She had already begun making her plan, but things changed when a group of women began to visit the jail on Monday evenings. They spoke and sang about Jesus, and they prayed with inmates one-on-one. A woman named Candice befriended Donna, prayed with her, and gave her a Bible, directing her to start reading in the book of John.

Donna figured she had nothing better to do with her time, so she did as Candice instructed. Reading God's Word took her back to her childhood. She recalled that her dad, whom she had seen only on weekends and during the summer, had introduced her to Jesus when she was eight years old. She had believed in God's existence since then, but she'd never understood what it meant to have a personal relationship with him—until now.

The women's weekly visits ignited Donna's faith. The more she read her Bible, the more peace she experienced in her soul. "I'd never known peace before, and I was like, whoa, this is awesome," she said.

Donna began to recognize God's prompts to pray for—and with—fellow inmates, and she saw answers to those prayers. Some women were released early, and others received their bond payments. Donna also saw God's hand at work in her own life. On one occasion, she received a check from a stranger—enough to buy needed toiletries and underwear. In her words, "God's provision blew my mind."

One day, she and two other inmates were talking about God and thanking him for his mercy and kindness. That's when she experienced a life-changing aha moment. "It was like God's Spirit came over me, and the eyes of my understanding were enlightened. I suddenly understood that I was free!" remarked Donna. "I could see how God saw me, and I didn't have to stay in turmoil anymore. I didn't have to stay in the same condition. John 8:32 came to mind, and I finally understood what Jesus meant when he said, 'You will know the truth, and the truth will set you free.' I was experiencing the freedom of God, even in the middle of all the stuff I was dealing with."

Donna was eventually sentenced to five years and ten months in another facility, with credit for the time she'd already served. Understandably, she didn't want to go, but the positive transformation in her thoughts—especially in the way she viewed herself—prepared her for the transition.

At the new facility, Donna broke her silence about the molestation she'd endured. For the first time, a confidante listened to her story, wrapped her in her arms, and let her cry. Counseling also helped her address the pain in her past and move to a greater level of freedom than she had already experienced.

Radiating Jesus's love, one of the prison officers also provided godly counsel whenever Donna had questions or needed advice. Several Christian inmates affirmed Donna as well and encouraged her to persevere when the going got rough. Bible study classes helped her dig into God's Word, and participating in a choir and on a praise dance team brought joy.

Donna admits that she once questioned what good could possibly come from the harsh reality of life behind bars. But in retrospect, she sees that this undistracted time gave her the opportunity to address her past and get to a healthy place mentally, emotionally, and spiritually. Understanding her identity as a daughter of the heavenly King helped her overcome shame, and learning about his love helped her embrace his forgiveness. Realizing that he created her for a purpose gave her meaning.

Donna's story proves the transformative power of *Yahweh Tzidkenu*. Today, she is a self-worth coach whose passion is to help women discover their value in God's eyes. She has written a book titled *Untarnished* to help others see themselves as God does when they are wrapped in his robe of righteousness.[3]

Everyone's circumstances are unique. You may or may not be able to relate to Donna's story, but I suspect you can relate to the feelings of shame she mentioned. I certainly can, and I'm so grateful that *Yahweh Tzidkenu* addresses this all-too-prevalent issue.

Yahweh Tzidkenu and Shame

Sometimes we speak about guilt and shame as though they're interchangeable, but that's not the case. *Guilt* is a feeling of regret for doing something wrong or failing to be proactive about doing the right thing. It arises from an action and motivates us to change our behavior.

For instance, let's say I'm a mom with young children. It's been a long day, and I need a few minutes of peace and quiet to recharge. Problem is, peace and quiet are not happening. The kids fight, the baby cries, the dog barks, the phone rings, and the saucepan boils over. So do I, and my kids take the heat. I immediately feel guilty for exploding, and the Holy Spirit nudges me to ask my kids for forgiveness. The unpleasant feelings associated with guilt motivate me to obey and think twice before behaving that way again.

Shame, however, is different:

> Shame is defined as a self-conscious emotion arising from the sense that something is fundamentally wrong about oneself. With shame, we often feel inadequate and full of self-doubt, yet these experiences may be outside of our conscious awareness.... Shame ... arises as a result of negative evaluations from others, even if we're just being ourselves. It's not so much that what we did is bad, but that who we are is bad. As a result, we may feel small, worthless, or powerless. Over time, shame can lead to something called the 'internalized other'—an image or idea that someone disapproves of us. We may then hold negative evaluations of ourselves through the eyes of others.[4]

Back to the motherhood example. Let's say my kids forgive me, but a nagging sense of shame lingers. It says no one else yells at their kids, so there must be something wrong with me. If people knew the real me, they'd call Social Services and suggest a visit to my home. I'm a bad mother who's ruining her kids.

With shame comes the fear that we're a disappointment to God. It often causes us to retreat or hide, just as Adam and Eve hid from God after choosing their way over his. And sometimes we strive to earn our way back into his good graces to influence his negative evaluation of us.

I speak from experience. For the most part, I played the role of a good Christian girl in my growing-up years, but I struggled with a deep sense of shame and worthlessness. As far as I can understand, the seed was planted when a neighbor's son molested me when I was six years old. I told no one. I was the victim, but shame said I was a bad person and deserved it.

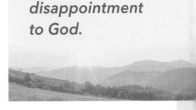

With shame comes the fear that we're a disappointment to God.

Shame silenced me for nearly six decades.

In my dating days, I made choices that left me feeling guilty and prompted me to change my behavior. Yet the shame lingered. Good Christian girls didn't do those things; therefore, I must be bad. Being sexually assaulted by someone I trusted compounded those feelings.

I felt inadequate, small, worthless, and full of self-doubt; but I hid my feelings well. Others may have assumed that I had it all together, but I felt broken on the inside. I asked God to forgive me, but I never felt forgiven. So I asked again. And again.

Finally, I discovered a way to influence what I thought was God's negative evaluation of me. After Gene and I got engaged, the time came to shop for my wedding dress. Back then, I was on staff at the same

Bible college I'd attended as a student. My responsibilities required me to drive into a nearby city one day for business, so I took advantage of the opportunity to look for a gown. My mother lived 120 miles away, and she would have met me there if I'd told her my plan. But I didn't. I kept it to myself. It was my way of hiding and retreating, but I didn't see it that way at the time.

Shame convinced me that I was unworthy to be a bride who wore white. I listened to shame's voice and believed that God was disappointed with me. To change what I thought was God's negative evaluation of me, I bought a champagne-colored dress. When Mom later asked me about my choice, I answered, "This color suits me."

My beliefs and behavior would have looked much different if I'd understood the character of God as *Yahweh Tzidkenu*. I'd grown up attending church twice every Sunday and again for midweek kids' club and youth group, and I'd gone to Christian summer camp and Bible college. But somehow I had missed the truth about Christ clothing me in his righteousness. Pastor Craig Groeschel writes,

> Shame usually follows a pattern—a cycle of self-recrimination
> and lies that claims life after life. First, we experience an
> intensely painful event. Second, we believe the lie that our
> pain and failure is *who we are*—not just something we've done,
> or had done to us—and we experience shame. And finally,
> our feelings of shame trap us into thinking that we can never
> recover—that, in fact, we don't even deserve to.[5]

Perhaps that's how the harlot who slipped into Simon the Pharisee's dinner party felt. After all, scandalous living was her trademark. She knew what others whispered behind her back. She saw them glance the other way when she approached. She saw them cross the street to avoid her as though her presence might contaminate them.

The woman knew Simon's room would be filled with men, but she wasn't seeking their attention. There was only one man on her mind. Only one man she longed to see.

Her face flushed as she crossed the room. She felt the stares, but this time she didn't care. She was done: Done with feeling like the walking dead. Done with drowning on the inside. Done with feeling like the dirt under her feet.

Only one man could pull her from the depths of despair.

She knelt at Jesus's feet and wept, her tears washing away the day's dust. She dried his feet with her hair, kissed them over and over, and poured expensive perfume on them.

Shame told the immoral woman that she didn't deserve God's love. She came to Jesus wounded and broken, destitute of hope and desperate for healing. Shame told her that her life was beyond redemption, but Jesus said otherwise: "Your sins are forgiven. Your faith has saved you; go in peace" (Luke 7:48, 50).

Some of us can relate to her despair. We've engaged in behaviors for which we condemn ourselves. We've made regrettable choices. We've tried to carry an unbearable burden of shame and battered ourselves with self-blame. We may feel like the worst of sinners, like we're at the end of ourselves with nowhere to go. We might feel unworthy, unlovable, and unforgivable. But, friend, *Yahweh Tzidkenu* changes everything.

Yahweh Tzidkenu: Power to Transform

As we already know, even people considered basically good by human standards fall short of God's standard of righteousness. Let's face it: There's just no way we can ever achieve it on our own.

That's why God sent his son, Jesus—to take our sin upon himself and give us his righteousness in exchange: "God made him who had no sin to be sin for us, so that in him we might become the righteousness of God" (2 Corinthians 5:21 NIV).

Tony Evans writes, "Just as our sin was credited to Jesus's account when He hung on the cross to die, His righteousness is credited to each one of us who trust in Him as our Lord and Savior." Evans illustrates this concept by using a bank account:

> If a bank teller called you today and said $10,000 was credited to your account, you would celebrate. You would get your praise dance on and shout a hallelujah because you could begin to make withdrawals from the credit in your account. The same is true for the [*tzedek*] that God has given each of us through Jesus Christ. This name of God not only gives you a perfect credit score in terms of your standing with Him in heaven, but also allows you to make "righteous" withdrawals here on earth.[6]

By sending Jesus to die on our behalf and then the Holy Spirit to live in us, *Yahweh Tzidkenu* took away our sin and gave us the very righteousness of Christ himself. "This means that anyone who belongs to Christ has become a new person. The old life is gone; a new life has begun!" (2 Corinthians 5:17).

This great exchange cost God dearly, but he makes it free for us. When we accept his generosity, he transforms us through his righteousness. We can kiss man-made religious rules goodbye and strip off our filthy, do-it-yourself righteousness rags.

I watched the transformation happen in my parents' lives as they accepted my non-Mennonite man as a son. One evening as Gene and I visited them a couple of months after our wedding, my dad looked at my husband and remarked, "If I'm going to learn how to play cribbage, I guess now is the time."

To my amazement, Dad then produced a new set of playing cards and said, "Teach me." Cribbage bonded their friendship. In fact, after my dad lost his mobility, playing this game gave him something fun and mind-stimulating to do with friends who visited him at home and later at his nursing home.

Mom and Dad loved Gene so much that, on one occasion, my mom told me, "Gene is the best thing that ever happened to you." My parents also became friends with my in-laws. I have fond memories of watching Dad and Gene's mom play—you guessed it—cribbage at our kitchen table. This transformation was beautiful to behold as religious rags fell away in exchange for God's righteous robe, and relationships became more important than rules.

How Shall We Respond?

Responding appropriately to *Yahweh Tzidkenu* begins with admitting our sinfulness and our need for his righteousness. "If we confess our sins, he is faithful and just and will forgive us our sins and purify us from all unrighteousness" (1 John 1:9 NIV).

Next, we ask God to grant us faith to trust him as we grow in our relationship with him. Without faith in him and his promises, we fall back into thinking we can rely on our ability to attain righteousness through man-made spirituality. That's not how it works:

> For the Scriptures tell us, "Abraham believed God, and God counted him as righteous because of his faith." When people work, their wages are not a gift, but something they have earned. But people are counted as righteous, not because of their work, but because of their faith in God who forgives sinners.

ROMANS 4:3–5

Finally, we become intentional about growing in our relationship with God. Second Timothy 2:22 says, "Run from anything that stimulates youthful lusts. Instead, pursue righteous living, faithfulness, love, and peace. Enjoy the companionship of those who call on the Lord with pure hearts."

We intentionally flee temptation, read and apply God's Word, talk with him in prayer, and seek fellowship with others of like mind. There are so many resources to help further our faith walk, so let's take advantage of them.

Above all, remember that God desires a relationship with you more than he desires you to become a master at religiosity. This quote by Craig Groeschel says it all:

> Religion highlights my efforts to do what is right. The gospel highlights what Christ has already done. Religion lures me to believe that if I obey God, he will love me. But the gospel shows me that because God loves me, I get to obey him. Religion puts the burden on us. We have to do what is right. A relationship with Christ puts the burden on him. And because of what he did for us, we get to do what is right. Instead of an obligation, our right living is a response to his gift. Giving Christ our whole lives is the only reasonable response to such love. There's nothing more we need to do. *Nothing.*[7]

Prayer

Yahweh Tzidkenu, I acknowledge that I could never earn right standing with you by my own merit. All my attempts to impress you or to earn your favor through good works are futile, so thank you for coming to my rescue. Thank you for removing my fear that I will be judged for not being good enough. Thank you for removing my shame. I am eternally grateful that you are my righteousness. Help me walk in the truth of this manifestation of your character, and transform me through the process. In Jesus's name, amen.

Points TO *Ponder*

1 **Read Isaiah 61:10.**

- What was Isaiah's response to God clothing him in a robe of righteousness?

- Compare this with the woman's actions in Luke 7:37-38.

- Which response can you most relate to, and why?

2 **Read 1 John 1:9 and Psalm 103:3.**

- Complete this sentence: God cleanses us from _____ unrighteousness.

- Why is it difficult for us to believe that "all" means "all"?

3 **Read Psalm 34:4-5.**

- What promise is given to those who look to God for help?

- How have you struggled with shame?

- How does understanding the name *Yahweh Tzidkenu* help move you beyond the fear of not being good enough for God?

4 **Read Ezekiel 36:26-27.**

- What wonderful actions has God taken to help us lead righteous lives?

- How have you experienced his righteousness at work in your life?

- How does the obedience mentioned here differ from obeying man-made religious rules?

5 Read Matthew 5:6 in either the ESV, NIV, NKJV, or NASB version of the Bible.

- What does it mean to "hunger and thirst for righteousness"?

- What promise is given to those who crave it?

- Rate your appetite for knowing God on a scale of 1 to 10 (with 10 being ravenous).

- Compare this verse with Matthew 6:33. How are you intentionally pursuing righteousness?

Scan the QR code or go to

hendricksonrose.org/ LivingUnafraidSession2

for more author insights about the name *Yahweh Tzidkenu*.

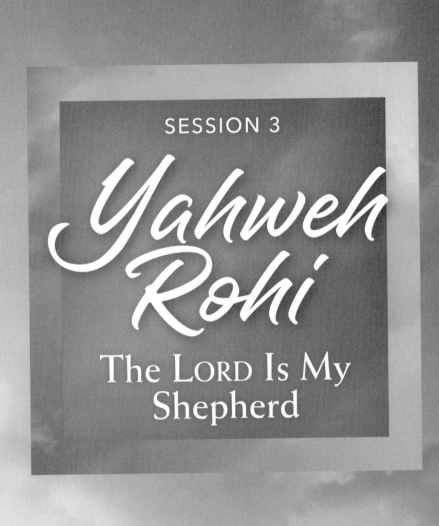

SESSION 3

Yahweh Rohi

The Lord Is My Shepherd

ON MY FIFTIETH BIRTHDAY, I sat in my backyard, soaking up the summer sun and sipping my morning coffee. With a half century of faith-filled adventures behind me, I looked forward to what the future held.

It seemed appropriate to celebrate the day with a spiritual marker of some sort, so I prayed, "God, thank you for your faithfulness in the past. As I turn this corner and enter a new phase, please give me a promise to carry me through the next fifty years."

Psalm 23:1 instantly came to mind: "The LORD is my shepherd; I have all that I need."

"Wow—thank you. That's perfect!" I said as I scribbled the Scripture in my journal.

Cut! Rewind.

That was not my response. Not even close.

I'm embarrassed to tell you the truth: I actually frowned and thought, *Thanks, but no thanks. That's too familiar. Too simple. Give me something with a little more pizzazz, please.*

I brushed the verse away and waited for a different download, but Psalm 23:1 returned with notable determination. I waved it away a second time, but my efforts failed. It landed once more, and this time, I let it stay.

Hindsight is a great teacher. Surprise, surprise—God knew what he was doing when he gave me Psalm 23:1. He knew my future held deep, dark valleys where I'd need a shepherd's encouragement to lead and love me along the way. Though I insisted on something different, I'm grateful he persisted. Hindsight is a great teacher.

Yahweh desires a close relationship with his people, and *Yahweh Tzidkenu* made this possible by becoming our righteousness. Now, experiencing him as a shepherd, as *my* shepherd (*Yahweh Rohi*), has changed my life.

It resuscitates me when fear and despair suck the breath from my lungs. It anchors my soul when life's storms batter me. It soothes me when disappointments dash my dreams to smithereens, and it assures me that all will be well, because my shepherd cradles me close to his heart.

Yahweh Rohi: What Does It Mean?

"The LORD [Yahweh] is my shepherd [Rohi]." It's easy to skim over these words without stopping to appreciate their depth and beauty, so let's press pause to explore this description of God as a shepherd.

As we learned in session 1, Bibles usually translate God's personal name, Yahweh, as "LORD," which refers to the self-existent, all-sufficient God who wants to engage with his creation.

The Hebrew word for shepherd is a form of the word ra-ah, a verb that means "to pasture, tend, graze, feed."[1] Ro-i, from which we get Rohi (pronounced "roh-EE"), is a possessive form and means "my shepherd."

Ra-ah can also mean "to associate with, be a friend of."[2] It denotes intimacy and implies that a shepherd cherishes the sheep in his care. The prophet Isaiah used it to describe God's tenderness toward his people: "He will feed his flock like a shepherd. He will carry the lambs in his arms, holding them close to his heart. He will gently lead the mother sheep with their young" (Isaiah 40:11).

A friend of mine demonstrates this kind of tenderness toward the lambs born on her hobby farm every spring. Knowing their muscles will strengthen with use, she lets them struggle to stand on their wobbly legs, but she tenderly scoops them up when she sees them tire. She cradles them in her arms, strokes their wool, and speaks encouragement over them. Such is the picture of Yahweh Rohi's care for us, his lambs.

The compound name Yahweh Rohi reveals God as the almighty Creator who cares deeply for us. But delving into the entire phrase, "The LORD is my shepherd," adds more insight. Between the key words at the beginning ("The LORD") and end ("shepherd"), we find two small but significant English words that add to this description of God.

First, *is*. While there is no verb used in the Hebrew phrase, the context suggests that it is set in the present tense, as our English translations show. Thus, *Yahweh Rohi* is a present-tense God. He is God of the now. He is current. He is relevant. And he is continually available, caring for us every moment of every day.

> The self-existent God who created and sustains the universe stoops to become our loving shepherd.

Second, *my*. *Ro-i*, a form of *ra-ah* with a first-person pronoun ending, specifically means "my shepherd." *My* defines *Yahweh Rohi* as a personal shepherd. David could have written, "The LORD is *a* shepherd," but that misses the mark.

Yahweh Rohi is not just any old generic shepherd; he is *my* shepherd, and he is *your* shepherd, and we are his sheep. He owns and cherishes us because he bought us with the precious blood of Jesus. We belong to him and are completely dependent upon him for everything, just as a sheep relies upon the shepherd. It's all about relationship.

Imagine! The self-existent God who created and sustains the universe stoops to become our loving shepherd. He cares for us, provides for us, and stands guard over us. He watches over us as we strengthen our faith muscles. He knows when we grow discouraged and fainthearted, and he's there to cradle us and speak encouragement over us. And that's just the beginning.

What Is Our Shepherd Like?

In 2018, my husband and I purchased a sailboat and made it our home, which meant parting with many of our earthly belongings. This included a picture that adorned our dining room wall. It featured a young woman clad in a flowing white dress and blue bonnet, lounging in the shade of a large tree while a dozen lambs and ewes grazed nearby. Everything about the scene sighed serenity, but it did not reflect the reality of a shepherd's life.

In Bible times, the job of shepherd was considered dirty and despicable. People looked upon shepherds with disdain and considered them uneducated and untrustworthy. I think it's fascinating, then, that one of the ways God manifests his character is by using a name that has a derogatory connotation.

Why would he do that? Why would he choose to exchange heaven's glory for life on earth among us—a bunch of senseless, defenseless human sheep? Why would he choose to lay down his life for our sake?

The name *Yahweh Rohi* explains the inexplicable: God loves us. As we learned by studying the meaning of *Yahweh*, he's not a distant deity who has abandoned us to figure things out on our own. Nor is he a big bully who wields a baseball bat and waits for us to botch things up. He is the almighty, sovereign God who created us and loves us and longs to lavish his care and goodness on us.

Understanding God's love is the first step toward overcoming fear. Believing by faith that he holds us close to his heart fills us with courage, and we can trust that he cares for us as a shepherd cares for his sheep, leading us to a place of sweet, quiet rest. It enables us to trust his sovereignty, especially when he allows us to experience difficult circumstances that defy comprehension.

I believe that our journey from fear to freedom is further strengthened when we embrace a few other qualities that *Yahweh Rohi* possesses.

1. *Yahweh Rohi* Is Wise

First, our shepherd is wise. Pastor and author A. W. Tozer defined wisdom as "the ability to devise perfect ends and to achieve those ends by the most perfect means. It sees the end from the beginning, so there can be no need to guess or conjecture."[3]

In the Bible, wisdom is often paired with knowledge, because having wisdom about a situation is based on knowing the facts. Since God knows everything about everything, he is fully wise. "By wisdom the LORD [*Yahweh*] founded the earth; by understanding he created the heavens. By his knowledge the deep fountains of the earth burst forth, and the dew settles beneath the night sky," says Proverbs 3:19–20.

Creation teems with examples of *Yahweh's* wisdom:

- The earth tilts on its axis at a 23.5-degree angle. This creates four seasons, without which life on earth would likely be impossible.

- Fluid in our ears helps with balance. When the fluid moves, it tells the brain how to compensate, and the brain responds by sending appropriate messages to the body.

- Bees build honeycombs by forming their wax into hexagon shapes. Who told them that hexagons are stronger than squares and triangles? Who taught them that compared to other shapes, hexagons hold more honey for the amount of wax used?

- Sunflowers warm up quickly by facing east. Their warmth in turn attracts pollinating insects. If this process fails to happen, the flower self-pollinates.

All of creation—from outer space to the intricacies of the human body, from bugs to blossoms, and everything in between—declares *Yahweh's* wisdom. He knows the outcome he wants to achieve, and he knows the best means of reaching that outcome. There's no guesswork, no doubt, and no uncertainty with him.

When waves of fear slosh around me, I remind myself that God knows everything about everything. Nothing takes my shepherd by surprise, and nothing leaves him baffled. He alone knows why he allows certain circumstances to happen, what he plans to accomplish through them, and how to do so in the most perfect way.

Our shepherd's wisdom cannot be measured. It's as infinite as the grains of sand that make up all the world's beaches and deserts combined. Comparatively, our wisdom is like a single grain of sand. Puny, right? It's no wonder Scripture declares, "Oh, how great are God's riches and wisdom and knowledge! How impossible it is for us to understand his decisions and his ways!" (Romans 11:33).

My friend, we'll never come close to knowing everything about everything, but we can choose to trust the one who does. Our shepherd is all-wise; he knows the solutions to our problems, and he never makes a mistake.

2. *Yahweh Rohi* Is Good

Second, our shepherd is good. He is always truly and fully good—in other words, perfect. The psalmist declared it in these words: "O LORD [*Yahweh*], your unfailing love fills the earth. You are good and do only good" (Psalm 119:64, 68).

Good through and through—that is who *Yahweh Rohi* is. He never does something intended for evil, since that would be contrary to his nature. Bad things happen because sin negatively affects our world, but he can turn something bad into something good and beneficial. I've witnessed this many times.

It happened on one occasion while I was sitting in a pediatric intensive care room with another young mom. Her son, born without a nose, was recovering from the first of many reconstructive facial surgeries, and my eleven-month-old daughter had just undergone brain surgery to remove a cyst. As mothers, we would have given anything to change our children's situations, but circumstances were beyond our control. They were not, however, beyond *Yahweh Rohi*'s control. He placed two moms and their infants in that room, and common circumstances forged a relationship.

My new friend felt desperately afraid for her son's future. With her permission, I told her that God's wisdom and goodness were my basis for hope, and I talked about God's love and his desire to be involved in her life. She listened intently and welcomed my prayers for her and her son. She knew that she could invite God to be her shepherd, and he would help her navigate the unknowns ahead.

Even if our worst fears become reality, we can hold on to hope for a good outcome, because God's Word says, "After you have suffered a little while, he will restore, support, and strengthen you, and he will place you on a firm foundation" (1 Peter 5:10). *Yahweh Rohi* is our good, good shepherd, and we can trust him. No. Matter. What.

3. *Yahweh Rohi* Is Strong

Third, our shepherd is strong. Consider the annual World's Strongest Man competition, where an event called "Power Stairs" requires participants to lift a series of three objects to the top of a flight of stairs. Each object weighs anywhere from four hundred to six hundred pounds. Another event requires contestants to manually pull a train car, transport truck, bus, or plane for one hundred feet, as fast as possible.

My mind can't fathom human strength of this caliber. It sounds impressive, but bulging muscles and ripped abs are nothing compared to our shepherd's strength. Imagine this: *Yahweh*'s finger—a mere finger—caused the third plague in Egypt (Exodus 8:19) and wrote the Old Testament law on stone tablets (Exodus 31:18). The most one of my fingers can muster is to point someone in the right direction and write a message in tabletop dust!

Yahweh Rohi parted the Red Sea and drowned the Egyptian army as they chased the Israelites (Exodus 14:26-31). He granted Hannah a son despite her struggles with infertility (1 Samuel 1:27). He delivered David from a lion, a bear, and the giant Goliath (1 Samuel 17:37, 50-51).

The list of *Yahweh Rohi*'s feats could go on and on, but you get the picture. We'll talk more about his strength and ability to do the impossible throughout this book, but for now, rest assured that anything is possible for our shepherd. Because of who he is, there's nothing he cannot do;

therefore, we can trust him when facing fearful impossibilities that tower over us like giants.

Yahweh Rohi's Role

On my first trip to Romania, Gene and I visited a husband-and-wife team of ministry coworkers living near the city of Timişoara. During our stay, we drove past a flock of sheep grazing beside the road, with their shepherd and a dog standing nearby, keeping a watchful eye.

I asked our host to stop the car so I could step outside and capture a close-up of the scene, but he warned against it. "The shepherd has trained that dog to protect the sheep," he replied. "It will rip you to shreds if he thinks you're a threat." Enough said.

Romanian shepherds are a hardy bunch who take their role seriously, because their reputation and livelihood depend on the flock's well-being. They brave extreme weather and endure separation from their families for up to five months, depending on where they find good grazing land. They live without electricity, running water, and plumbing and sometimes sleep in a structure that resembles a man-sized rabbit hutch.

Good shepherds take all measures necessary to ensure their sheep remain healthy.

Good shepherds willingly sacrifice personal comfort and take all measures necessary to ensure their sheep remain healthy. They lead the flock to pastureland and ensure a safe space for the animals to rest without fear of predators attacking them. They provide clean drinking water, care for the sick and wounded, and search for those that wander from the flock. That's quite a job description, and it resembles the tasks that *Yahweh Rohi* performs on our behalf. Let's take a peek at four of them.

1. *Yahweh Rohi* Quenches Our Thirst

If a shepherd fails to ensure that his animals have clean drinking water to stay properly hydrated, the sheep will settle for anything wet to quench their thirst. Dirty water? No problem. Contaminated? Sure, why not? Drinking from these sources leaves the critters at risk for parasites and disease, but that doesn't stop them from making the wrong move.

God created us to thirst after him (Psalm 42:1-2). He then supplied us with the purest source of spiritual water in the person of Jesus, who said, "Let anyone who is thirsty come to me and drink" (John 7:37 NIV). Trouble is, like sheep, we're not always the brightest on the block. Our human bent thinks we know better, so we set out to quench our thirst using other sources.

We run to human relationships, social media, money, hobbies, alcohol, drugs, or sex. We turn to power, position, and material possessions. We travel, volunteer, and campaign for good causes. But none of these work, because they're cheap substitutes for the real thing. Only Jesus satisfies our spiritually thirsty souls, and *Yahweh Rohi* has made that provision.

2. *Yahweh Rohi* Comforts Us in the Valleys

I suspect that throughout world history, few words have brought more solace to the dying and to those in danger than these: "Yea, though I walk through the valley of the shadow of death, I will fear no evil: for thou art with me; thy rod and thy staff they comfort me" (Psalm 23:4 KJV).

The Hebrew word that is often translated "shadow of death" is used eighteen times in the Bible, with more than half of those occurrences in the book of Job. The term denotes the worst scenario imaginable, where "valley" evokes imagery of being surrounded or even trapped by obstacles, perhaps with no way of escape. Put together, "the valley of the shadow of death" means the absolute worst imaginable situation.

I walked through my deepest, darkest valley (to date) after giving birth in Nepal to our second child, Stephanie. Gene and I had moved there in July 1982 as newlyweds. Our heart's desire was to volunteer with a

Christian nonprofit organization, where Gene could use his engineering degree to work on a hydroelectric power project. Our son, Matthew, was born a year later, and Stephanie arrived when he was twenty months old.

Our wee daughter was born with hydrocephalus—too much cerebral fluid on the brain. Doctors suspected other physical issues as well, but the hospital lacked proper equipment to assess Stephanie's needs and provide help. "You must return to North America on the first available flight," we were told.

That was Tuesday, March 19. The next day, Gene tried to buy tickets for Friday's flight. When the booking agent learned that I'd had a cesarean delivery and Stephanie was only a day old, he said, "Your wife is a medical high risk, so she'll have to wait at least a week to fly. Besides, we don't want an infant less than two weeks old aboard the plane."

Gene devised a plan and bought a ticket for himself. On Thursday, we drove by Land Rover twelve hours to Kathmandu, and on Friday morning, he visited the American embassy to secure a passport for Stephanie. Mission accomplished, he wrapped her in a big blanket, threw a diaper bag over his shoulder, took a baby bottle filled with mom's milk, and headed to the airport.

I remained behind with Matthew. My body felt wrecked by the C-section and the long, windy, bumpy ride to Kathmandu. Now my heart felt broken and afraid. What would happen to Stephanie? Would she live or die? If she lived, what would her quality of life look like?

Our missionary career appeared to have ended. Was this merely a temporary setback or a permanent change? What did our family's future hold? We had no idea—only that we were headed back to the United States with no job awaiting my husband. We had no car, no home, and no health insurance. How in the world would we pay the bills for neonatal intensive care? We faced the absolute worst imaginable scenario.

Deep, shadowy valleys are scary places for sheep, because the sheep lack visual depth perception and can't see what lurks in the dark. Even in the light, they're naturally nervous creatures. Rowdy dogs, sudden noises, and strangers frighten them; and the sight of a wolf, bear, or fox puts them into panic mode. They're defenseless and depend on their fellow sheep for protection, so becoming separated from the flock terrifies them.

When a sheep feels afraid, its heart rate increases, and because it cannot fight, it chooses the flight response. It might trample other sheep in its attempt to run away, and a pregnant ewe might miscarry. The sheep remains in a heightened state of stress until the source of perceived danger is removed.

The shepherd knows best how to minimize his sheep's stress. He approaches it within its line of vision and speaks in a calm voice. If a corner of the barn is dark, he either leads the way or shines a light into the shadows to show the animal there is nothing to be afraid of. If the shepherd must isolate a sheep, he ensures that it can always see the flock. Whatever the cause for fear, the shepherd does his best to address the source of the problem so his sheep can live free from fear's harmful effects.

On that most memorable day in Nepal, *Yahweh Rohi* understood my fears and came to my rescue. I recall holding my toddler close and letting my tears flow. "What is happening?" I whispered to God. "What do you want me to learn?" He answered by bringing to mind the lyrics of a hymn I'd known since childhood:

> *Great is Thy faithfulness, O God my Father;*
> *There is no shadow of turning with Thee;*
> *Thou changest not, Thy compassions, they fail not;*
> *As Thou hast been, Thou forever wilt be.*
>
> *Great is Thy faithfulness!*
> *Great is Thy faithfulness!*
> *Morning by morning new mercies I see;*
> *All I have needed Thy hand hath provided;*
> *Great is Thy faithfulness, Lord, unto me!*[4]

I didn't know what the future held, but I knew who held me. He didn't promise Stephanie's survival, but he guaranteed his presence and faithfulness. Embraced in my shepherd's arms, I knew that everything would be okay, even if the outcome was different from what I was hoping for.

Life gives us more than enough reasons to fear. Storms hit and thrash our little boat until we begin believing we'll not survive the turbulence. But God understands exactly how we feel and why. In some cases, he removes us from the scary situation or provides a quick resolution. In others, he allows us to linger in that place, but he never leaves us alone, and he always gives us the strength to persevere.

When fear rises in me—especially the fear of an unknown future and fear for my loved ones' well-being—I call Psalm 34:4–5 to mind: "I prayed to the Lord, and he answered me. He freed me from all my fears. Those who look to him for help will be radiant with joy; no shadow of shame will darken their faces."

Where we set our sights when we feel afraid is a choice we make. Focusing on our circumstances magnifies our fear, but focusing on our shepherd sets us free. We can trust him, because he comforts us in the valleys.

3. *Yahweh Rohi* Restores Our Souls

Years ago, a discarded dresser caught my eye. Covered with grime and chipped white paint, it sat forlorn and forgotten in an old dormitory room. I couldn't resist when it called my name, so I brought it home and set to work restoring it.

Stripping layers of old paint revealed the dresser's lovely wood grain, and I began to see its full potential. I sanded its surfaces and applied Swedish oil. With a finishing flair, I exchanged the old knobs for new ones. Presto! Once tossed aside, the dresser assumed the new purpose of holding my kitchen linens, while guests in my dining room could enjoy its beauty. Restoring anything takes hard work, but the result is worth the effort.

A shepherd who rescues a sheep from a "cast" position would agree. A cast sheep is one that has rolled onto its back and cannot right itself. Its feet flail as the animal lies there, frustrated and helpless. Eventually, gases build up and expand in part of the sheep's stomach, cutting off blood circulation to the legs. The sheep will die within hours, unless the shepherd finds it first.

When a shepherd sees a cast sheep, he slowly rolls it onto its side to relieve the gas pressure. He then lifts the animal to its feet—sometimes propping it between his own legs for support—and massages its extremities to restore circulation. He continues his tender work until the animal stands unassisted and finally runs off to rejoin the flock.

Sometimes the human soul, like an old dresser or a cast sheep, needs restoration too (Psalm 23:3). The reasons are many, including sin.

King David knew all about it. He abused his position when he slept with Bathsheba and then arranged for her husband's death to cover his tracks (2 Samuel 11:2–17). David's sin cast his soul into a position of guilt and joylessness, but *Yahweh Rohi* sought his wayward sheep by sending the prophet Nathan to confront him. Thankfully, David responded well. He confessed his sin to God and took responsibility for his actions. "Restore to me the joy of your salvation, and make me willing to obey you," he prayed (Psalm 51:12).

The Good Shepherd was faithful to forgive and set his cast sheep back on his feet. In Psalm 32:10–11, we hear the sound of a restored soul in David's voice: "Many sorrows come to the wicked, but unfailing love surrounds those who trust the LORD. So rejoice in the LORD and be glad, all you who obey him! Shout for joy, all you whose hearts are pure!"

Nothing much has changed since David's day. Sin still casts down our souls: anger, jealousy, unforgiveness, greed, lust, pride, and self-reliance set us on our backs, metaphorically speaking. It drains our spiritual vitality and makes us easy prey for the enemy of our souls. Thankfully, *Yahweh Rohi* sees our condition and provides the way of rescue through the person of Jesus Christ.

Difficult circumstances can leave us flailing too. My daughter Stephanie's first two years of life led our family through several deep, dark valleys. After our sudden return to North America to address her medical needs, she underwent a dozen surgeries for various reasons and survived a bout with meningitis, which was misdiagnosed twice by medical professionals.

Gene and I were strangers in our new community and lived far from our parents, so finding childcare for Matthew proved challenging when I had to sit with Stephanie at the hospital. Gene did double duty—after work, he relieved me at the hospital so I could fetch Matthew, feed him dinner, and put him to bed. Life was hard and stress ran high, but in retrospect I understand the many ways that *Yahweh Rohi* cared for us and worked to restore our souls:

- He provided Gene with a civil engineering job only two weeks after our return from Nepal.

- He brought our plight to the attention of an organization that covered Stephanie's medical expenses for the first year.

- He nudged friends to donate money so we could buy a car.

- He prompted a local journalist to write about our story. When an older couple read the article, they invited us to house-sit for several months, which gave us time to find a repossessed mobile home within our paltry budget.

- We began attending a nearby church, and the congregation adopted us. One grandmother offered to babysit Matthew occasionally, and the pastor's wife showed up at the hospital to hold Stephanie on a particularly difficult day. During that same hospital stay, another woman from the church took me out for lunch while Stephanie slept.

Yahweh Rohi knows our needs. He sees us when we grow weary, and he meets us in that place. He sets us back on our feet and tenderly works to restore us and strengthen us for the road ahead. Evangelist David Wilkerson put it this way:

> [Yahweh Rohi] is not some doting, passive shepherd. He is not a hireling—someone who just provides food and guidance. He does not merely point us toward the grassy pasture and pools of water and say, "There's what you need. Go and get it." Nor does He turn a blind eye to our needs. He does not walk the other way when He hears our cries for help and sees us in trouble. No, He knows every pain we endure, every tear we shed and every hurt we feel. He knows when we are too weary to go another step. He knows just how much we can take. Most of all, He knows how to rescue us and bring us to a place of healing.[5]

So beautiful, yes?

4. *Yahweh Rohi* Prepares a Banquet for Us

Being involved in missions allows me to travel internationally, and a favorite aspect of this opportunity is receiving an invitation to someone's home. Perhaps the most memorable one came in 2018 when we returned to the Nepalese village where we'd served in the 1980s.

Two years earlier, Gene and I had become Facebook friends with a couple of the villagers, which allowed us to let them know we were coming for a visit. On the day we arrived, the village leader and his wife ushered us into their mud-and-rock home and placed dishes of rice and lentils before us. This was remarkable since they belong to the highest Hindu caste, and we belong to no caste. According to their belief system, our presence in their house would defile it.

Yet they didn't seem to mind. After a delightful visit, the leader accompanied us to the next house, where more food awaited. And so it went throughout the entire village: From house to house, food was shared between friends from vastly different cultures, serving as a catalyst to rekindle memories, ignite conversations, and reestablish emotional connections.

Sharing food is a global relationship-based activity, which may explain the significance of King David's reference in Psalm 23 to what *Yahweh Rohi* does for him: "You prepare a table before me in the presence of my enemies" (verse 5 NIV). The verb tense for "prepare" indicates an ongoing action, meaning that God continuously meets our emotional needs for relationship with him. He never leaves us to rely on yesterday's leftovers.

The Hebrew word translated as "before" is *panim*, which means "face"— the literal front of a person. David is implying that *Yahweh*, his shepherd, is preparing a meal while face-to-face with him. *Yahweh Rohi* neither turns his back nor leaves the room, even momentarily. He's fully present and committed to the one on whom he lavishes attention.[6]

> *Even if things don't turn out as you hope, your enemies don't stand a chance because you're in the shepherd's presence and care.*

Now, here's where it gets really good. The meal *Yahweh Rohi* prepares isn't spread in a quiet corner at a table for two or on a private deck overlooking the sea. On the contrary, the shepherd and his sheep sit down to eat in a room filled with "enemies"—a translation of a form of the Hebrew word that can mean "to show hostility toward" or "to be cramped." The

foes to which David refers might be thought of as those who are trying to choke or suffocate him.[7]

Enemies wanting to squeeze the life from David surround him and *Yahweh Rohi*, but the shepherd doesn't banish them from the room. Why bother when they can't bother him? *Yahweh Rohi* doesn't give them a second thought, because his presence renders them powerless.

As for David, he's aware that his enemies are there, but he chooses not to fear them, because he knows the shepherd is on his side. He's in good company, in good hands. Why, then, should he be afraid?

Friend, *Yahweh Rohi* loves you as deeply as he loved King David. Fear over lack of finances might threaten to crush you. Fear for your loved ones' well-being might threaten to suffocate you. But remember this: Even if things don't turn out as you hope, these enemies don't stand a chance because you're in the shepherd's presence and care. Don't be afraid; he's got your back.

Jesus, Our Good Shepherd

Jesus declared himself to be "the good shepherd" who "sacrifices his life for the sheep" (John 10:11), an allusion to the many Old Testament passages that speak of God as a faithful shepherd. He loves us too much to leave us flailing in our sin.

He pursues us, sets us back on our feet, and gives us renewed purpose; but we must be willing to accept his help and means of restoration—that is, confession and forgiveness. "If we confess our sins to him, he is faithful and just to forgive us our sins and to cleanse us from all wickedness" (1 John 1:9).

Jesus also loves us too much to leave us flailing alone amid difficult circumstances. He is with us. He hears our cries, and he carries us close to his heart. Just as a real-life shepherd values the sheep within his care, so Jesus values us. He voluntarily laid down his life for our sake, to rescue us from Satan, the wolf who stalks and seeks to destroy us (John 10:11–12, 15, 18).

As a real-life shepherd earnestly pursues a sheep that has gone astray, so Jesus pursues the lost soul for the purpose of drawing him into the sheepfold, into that relationship for which God created him (John 10:16). And as a real-life shepherd knows his sheep individually and leads them along pathways that ensure their well-being, so Jesus calls us by name as he leads and guides us along the best pathways for our lives (John 10:3, 10).

Let's hold on to these truths when Satan tries to plant fearful thoughts in our minds. Jesus is our strong and caring shepherd, and we are his sheep. There's no safer place to be than cradled in his arms and under his watchful care.

How Shall We Respond?

The name *Yahweh Rohi* is simple but profound. It's worth meditating on to truly appreciate its depth, so here's an exercise to try.

First, speak the name aloud: "*Yahweh Rohi*—the LORD is my shepherd."

Repeat it thoughtfully four times, emphasizing a different key word each time. Begin with "LORD"—"The LORD is my shepherd."

Next, emphasize "is"—"The LORD *is* my shepherd."

Then, "The LORD is *my* shepherd."

And finally, "The LORD is my *shepherd*."

Take a few moments to ponder each key word and its relevance to the challenges you currently face.

Now take this exercise a step further and say aloud, "The LORD is *my* loving shepherd, and he quenches my thirst, comforts me in the darkest valley, restores my soul, and prepares a banquet for me."

Declare these truths the moment a fearful thought pops into your head. Rather than letting the anxious thought linger, use it as a trigger to praise God for being wise, good, and strong amid your challenges. I guarantee that fear will soon lose its grip.

Recalling the truth about *Yahweh Rohi*'s role calms our anxiety when headlines scream nothing but bad news on a national or global scale.

It helps us choose faith over fear when we watch a loved one struggle with chronic pain day in and day out.

It gives us courage when the car needs repairs, the kids need winter coats, and the furnace needs to be replaced—all at the same time.

What situation causes you to feel afraid today? Identify it, and then complete this sentence: "The LORD is my shepherd; and he is loving, wise, good, and strong. I choose to trust *Yahweh Rohi,* even when I feel afraid about _____."

Prayer

Yahweh Rohi, I praise you for being loving, wise, good, and strong. Because of who you are, I can trust you and know that everything is going to be okay. Thank you for quenching my thirst, comforting me in the valleys, restoring my soul, and preparing a table for me in the presence of my enemies. I can enjoy living unafraid because I am safe in your arms, cradled close to your heart. Help me walk in the truth of this manifestation of your character, and transform me through the process. In Jesus's name, amen.

Points TO Ponder

1 Which one of the key words in the phrase "The LORD is my shepherd" resonates most with you at this time, and why?

2 Read John 10:11 and John 10:14.

- Who is the speaker?

- How many times does he repeat the word *good?*

- How have you experienced his goodness in your life?

3 **Now read John 10:11 and John 10:15.**

■ What phrase is repeated in these verses?

■ What does it imply about the shepherd's commitment to our well-being?

4 **Read Ezekiel 34:11-12.**

■ What do these verses reveal about our shepherd's love for us?

■ How have you experienced his rescue amid tough circumstances?

5 Psalm 34:4 says, "I prayed to the Lord, and he answered me. He freed me from all my fears."

■ First, write a list of your fears.

■ Now read Isaiah 40:11. How does the truth in this verse help calm your fears?

Scan the QR code or go to

**hendricksonrose.org/
LivingUnafraidSession3**

for more author insights about
the name *Yahweh Rohi*.

SESSION 4

Yahweh Yireh

The LORD Will Provide

MOVING OUR FAMILY from Washington State to Quadra Island, British Columbia, where we would spend eleven years working at the Christian camp I mentioned in session 1, was no small decision. We had bathed this possibility in prayer for nearly nine years until we sensed the freedom to pursue it.

Gene left his lucrative civil engineering career, and we put our custom-built four-year-old lakefront house on the market. We packed our possessions, withdrew our kids from their school, bid goodbye to our friends and church family, and lumbered north with a loaded U-Haul.

Gene volunteered as an unpaid intern for six months, and then he was offered the position of program director. This role was also unpaid, so we began to develop a financial support team. Since online payments and e-transfers didn't exist in those days, we relied on our donors to mail their checks.

Who could have guessed that the Canadian postal service would launch a full-blown strike a few months after we started raising support? My already-limited grocery budget dwindled almost overnight, and staring into my bare cupboards, I felt like Old Mother Hubbard.

Three months earlier, we had become acquainted with a couple who'd brought their family to the camp for a week's vacation. We felt an instant connection, so we invited them to visit us in the fall, after our busy summer ministry ended. The earliest our schedules merged was in late November, so we set a date—and guess what? It happened to be during the postal strike.

The thought of preparing a nice meal with limited resources for ten people knotted my stomach, but neither Gene nor I felt okay about canceling our get-together. I cooked a pot of pasta, thawed a pound of hamburger, and did my best to stretch the fixings to feed the small crowd.

When our friends arrived, I stood outside to visit with the wife for a few minutes. From the corner of my eye, I saw the kids walking back and forth between their van and our back door, and I wondered what they were up to. My curiosity was satisfied when I went inside and—to my utter amazement—found bags of groceries piled on the kitchen counter!

Gene and I had told no one about our financial plight because, frankly, we felt embarrassed to admit our need. But we'd prayed, and now we were witnessing God's answer.

"I work at a grocery store," said the husband. "Yesterday I sensed God nudging me to buy groceries for you, so we did."

The bags held oatmeal and cold cereals, peanut butter, sugar, flour, and fresh fruits and vegetables—enough to fix a fine salad for that night's supper. They also contained goodies like chocolate chips, cheese, and fancy crackers for the soon-approaching Christmas season—items I could not have afforded that year.

I heartily agree with this statement by David Wilkerson: "Almost all new discoveries of God—all fresh revelations of His Person, nature, and character—are tied to some crisis, some intense human experience."[1]

Facing bare cupboards and a nearly empty fridge was an intense human experience for me, but that crisis became an unforgettable opportunity to discover God as *Yahweh Yireh*, my provider, and I wouldn't trade that lesson for all the cheese and fancy crackers in the world.

Yahweh Yireh: What Does It Mean?

For most of my life, I assumed the name *Yahweh Yireh* (pronounced "yeer-EH") only meant "God will provide." Knowing this gave me confidence when expressing my needs to him in prayer. But my appreciation for this name grew when I learned that in Hebrew the root word for *Yireh* means "to see, look at, inspect, perceive, consider."[2]

Yahweh Yireh is a provider extraordinaire. He sees our needs in advance and then sees to it that they are met at precisely the right time—not a moment too soon and not a moment too late. He also perceives our feelings about those needs. He's aware of the fears that cause sleepless nights and knotted stomachs. And because he promises to never leave or forsake us, we can rest assured that he is present with us in these situations. God experiences what we experience.

The name *Yahweh Yireh* reveals God's ability and willingness to supply our needs, but like the name *Yahweh*, it also infers a deeply personal relationship. And as *Yahweh Rohi*, our good shepherd, he is not a vending machine that spits out whatever we want on demand. Neither is he like a genie in a bottle who grants our wishes upon request.

Rather, he is the almighty God who knows our needs in advance, perceives our thoughts and feelings about those needs, and enters our experience with us as he provides for them.

No one knows this truth more intimately than the Old Testament hero Abraham.

Abraham Discovers God as *Yahweh Yireh*

The Bible contains only one usage of *Yahweh Yireh*—in Genesis 22, when Abraham faced the test of his life. Decades earlier, when Abraham was seventy-five years old and childless, God had promised to make him the father of a great nation (Genesis 12:2–4). But God didn't fulfill his promise immediately; Abraham waited twenty-five years for the birth of his son Isaac (Genesis 21:5).

One day when Isaac was a young man, God gave Abraham a bewildering command: "Take your son, your only son—yes, Isaac, whom you love so much—and go to the land of Moriah. Go and sacrifice him as a burnt offering on one of the mountains, which I will show you" (Genesis 22:2).

No one would have blamed Abraham for saying, "You must be kidding. Can we talk about this?" But Abraham didn't balk. He woke the next morning, loaded his donkey, gathered two servants and his beloved son, and cut enough firewood for a burnt offering. Then the foursome began a three-day trek to the mystery mountain in Moriah.

On the final leg of the sixty-mile hike, Isaac asked, "Where is the sheep for the burnt offering?" (Genesis 22:7). Perhaps Abraham wondered the same thing. If so, he didn't let on. Without a shred of drama or fanfare, he answered, "God will provide a sheep for the burnt offering, my son" (verse 8).

That's exactly what happened. *Yahweh Yireh* foresaw the need for a sacrificial sheep and provided it at precisely the right time—not a moment too soon and not a moment too late:

> *Abraham picked up the knife to kill his son as a sacrifice. At that moment the angel of the* Lord *called to him from heaven, "Abraham! Abraham!"*
>
> *"Yes," Abraham replied. "Here I am!"*
>
> *"Don't lay a hand on the boy!" the angel said. "Do not hurt him in any way, for now I know that you truly fear God. You have not withheld from me even your son, your only son."*
>
> *Then Abraham looked up and saw a ram caught by its horns in a thicket. So he took the ram and sacrificed it as a burnt offering in place of his son.*
>
> GENESIS 22:10–13

Perhaps, as Abraham climbed one side of the mountain, the ram was climbing the other. God was somehow working behind the scenes, doing his part as Abraham walked in obedience and faith. God perceived that Abraham *believed* he would become the father of many nations, and God entered into this intense human experience with his servant.

The sight of the ram snagged in the bushes gave Abraham a fresh revelation of God's character that unforgettable day, so "Abraham named the place Yahweh-Yireh (which means 'the Lord will provide'). To this day, people still use that name as a proverb: 'On the mountain of the Lord it will be provided'" (Genesis 22:14).

The sight of the groceries sitting on my kitchen counter did the same for me. Intellectual assent about God's ability to provide suddenly became real-life application. Understanding that God foresees my needs, perceives my thoughts and feelings about them, and experiences my crises with me has freed me from paralyzing fear.

Yahweh Yireh's prevision leads to provision.

The moment I feel my stress rise, I bring my request to *Yahweh Yireh* in prayer: "I know you can and will provide. How are you going to do it this time?" His answer might not look like what I expect or wish, but he never disappoints.

Perhaps your experience is like mine, and faith in *Yahweh Yireh* has brought you to a place of inner rest about your needs being met. Or maybe you're reading these words and thinking, *If only!*

If that is the case, then let me encourage you, my friend, with the truth that *Yahweh Yireh*'s *pre*vision leads to *pro*vision. Turn your focus away from your needs and onto his beautiful face, and confident expectation will replace your fear, as it has mine.

Yahweh Yireh Provides on Time

As Genesis 22 so beautifully portrays, God not only knows in advance what our needs will be but also supplies what is needed at precisely the right time. I, too, have repeatedly witnessed this miracle of God's just-on-time provision.

When our eldest daughter, Stephanie, chose to attend Bible college following her high school graduation, Gene and I supported her decision but had no clue how to pay for tuition and the extra expenses involved with attending a school far from home.

We prayed. We fasted. We thanked God in advance for what he would do. And then we watched with anticipation. How would he provide this time?

One afternoon in late summer, our kids' principal called to pose a question: "A student named Anna has applied to attend the school, but she doesn't live locally. She needs a place to stay during the week but will go home on weekends. She'll be in the same class as your youngest daughter, and I think they'll get along well. Would you consider letting her live with you in exchange for room and board?"

We decided to meet with Anna and her parents, and after giving the matter some thought and prayer, we said yes. Anna moved into our home on the same weekend Stephanie left for college, and that's when Anna's parents handed us the first check for her living expenses—not a moment too soon and not a moment too late.

Anna lived with us until she graduated from high school two years later, and her room and board payments went directly into Stephanie's account during that time. Steph's part-time job, scholarships, budgeting savvy, and willingness to live with a roommate in a basement suite worked together to make up the difference.

When Steph graduated, she was debt-free, and *Yahweh Yireh* deserves all the credit. His provision for Stephanie's college expenses was impeccable, and it came in a way we couldn't have foreseen. He's good at what he does, even though his math sometimes doesn't compute for us. If I could, though, I'd ask him why he often provides at the last minute— what I call "the midnight hour": Rent money arrives on the day rent comes due. Groceries show up when the cupboards are bare. Gas money appears when the empty tank needs to be filled. A ram appears when the knife is poised and ready to plunge.

What's with that? Why not ease our pressure by providing well in advance for the needs he knows we're going to face? If God had provided our family with a cash surplus months before Stephanie left for school, we could have lived with confidence that paying the college bills would be easy-peasy. No sweat.

But here's the thing: Knowing that my human nature leans toward independence and has a flawed perspective, I'm certain I would have placed my confidence in the cash surplus rather than in the person of *Yahweh Yireh*.

Not having a surplus led me to a place of utter dependence on the Lord. It forced me to face and surrender my fears. It kept me on my knees and grew my relationship with him. And in the end, I enjoyed the privilege of experiencing his faithfulness. Again.

"God meets daily needs daily. Not weekly or annually," says pastor and author Max Lucado. "He will give you what you need when it is needed."[3]

Yahweh Yireh's responsibility is to see to it that our needs are met at just the right time. Our role is to trust him in the process, although that's often easier said than done. When we're cast on the Lord to provide a certain something for us, we might grow impatient or let fear prompt us to jerk the wheel from his hands. Our emotions can step in and tell us that waiting and watching is futile. Clearly God needs our help, so we had best lend a helping hand. Yet that response never goes well.

Abraham learned this lesson the hard way when his wife, Sarah, grew weary of waiting for God to provide the son he'd promised. She decided to help him by arranging for her servant, Hagar, to sleep with Abraham (Genesis 16:1-4). According to that culture and time, the child conceived would legally belong to Sarah.

A son was born, but not the one God had promised. The connection Sarah shared with Hagar turned testy, and Sarah later discarded her servant and the child like pieces of unwanted property (Genesis 21:8-10). So much heartache could have been avoided if Sarah had trusted God to provide in his way and time.

I suspect Abraham learned never to take matters into his own hands again. I also suspect that seeing God provide a son through Sarah's womb, despite the physical impossibilities, laid the foundation for him to trust God to provide the sheep for the sacrifice on Mount Moriah, even if that provision didn't show up until the midnight hour.

No doubt Abraham's life would have been easier during that three-day trek if God had placed a sheep somewhere along their path, or at the base of the mountain, or in a thicket moments after Abe placed the wood on the altar.

But that's not the way *Yahweh Yireh* works. He waited until the precise moment when Abraham was about to sacrifice Isaac before placing the ram in Abraham's sight.

Abraham's implicit trust begs us to believe that God will provide for us, too, when he asks us to do something. He will see to it that we have everything needed. We can trust him, even if we must wait until the last minute, because he is, after all, *Yahweh Yireh*—the one whose provision comes with impeccable timing. Always.

Cyndi's Story: Discovering Deep Purpose

The name *Yahweh Yireh* is often associated with our physical needs, but that's just the beginning. His provision covers much more territory. My friend Cyndi Desjardins Wilkens is living proof.

As a successful sales manager and the mother of a five-year-old daughter and a newborn son, life was good for Cyndi and her family—until it took a detour when she developed flu-like symptoms that turned into renal failure, septic shock, and necrotizing fasciitis (flesh-eating disease).

Doctors placed her in a medically induced coma and told her husband that she would not survive, but Cyndi proved them wrong when she woke up five weeks later, albeit to a new reality. The medical professionals had saved her life, but they'd amputated her hands and feet in the process. Her daughter was afraid of her, and her son didn't remember her.

As Cyndi lay in her hospital bed, she cried rivers of tears and wrestled with God. "I'm a good person," she said, "so why would you allow this to happen to me? How can I live like this?" God provided answers by sending a nurse into her room, Bible in hand.

The nurse asked for permission to read it and then opened to Psalm 139. Cyndi listened and found comfort in words that reassured her of God's presence and sovereignty in her life.

In that moment, an image of being formed in her mother's womb with deep love and purpose came to mind. But Cyndi reasoned that the only way she could overcome the challenges ahead and see that purpose fulfilled was with the strength God could provide. That day, Cyndi placed her faith in Jesus and invited him to take control of her life. In her words, "Jesus picked up the pieces of my broken heart and put them back together."

When I invited Cyndi to share her story with our Bible study group, I specifically asked her to tell us how she'd experienced God as *Yahweh Yireh*. Her testimony illustrates the scope of his provision for us:

- **■ *Yahweh Yireh* provides hope.** Immediately after Cyndi was hospitalized and the doctors told her husband, Marc, to expect the worst, he began to read a Bible he had found in the waiting room. That's when he placed his faith in Jesus for salvation and started to pray for his wife's recovery. Marc's trust in God's ability to do a miracle gave Cyndi hope when she woke up from the coma and learned she would face life without her hands and feet. She cried buckets of tears, but she also found hope in God's promise to wipe away those tears someday.

- **■ *Yahweh Yireh* provides emotional and physical strength.** Cyndi had to relearn how to do basic tasks: brushing her teeth, combing her hair, feeding and dressing herself, changing her son's diapers. She acknowledges that her ability to persevere came from God. He provided her with the strength and tenacity to try and try again until her efforts yielded success.

- **■ *Yahweh Yireh* provides courage.** Most people told Cyndi she would never drive again, but she refused to believe them. She spent nine months training to drive, and the day finally came when she sat behind the steering wheel by herself. She looked toward the heavens in awe at what God had enabled her to accomplish.

"People say I'm courageous, but really, I'm not," Cyndi told our group. "The truth is, I don't have to be courageous, because *Yahweh Yireh* gives me courage. Like the psalmist wrote, 'When I am afraid, I put my trust in you. In God, whose word I praise'" (Psalm 56:3–4 NIV).

- *Yahweh Yireh* **brings healing.** Over time, Cyndi's body recovered from the initial trauma it had endured, but her new normal brought ongoing daily challenges. *Yahweh Yireh* continually gives Cyndi the strength needed to face the challenges that life with prosthetic hands and feet brings.

  She healed emotionally, too, as her relationship with Jesus grew. Discovering her identity in him set her free from striving for everything society said she must be, and she stopped hiding behind shame that dictated she somehow deserved this. She also realized that her friends could not heal her emotional wounds; only Jesus could do that. So she surrendered those hurts to him.

The women in my Bible study listened to Cyndi's story, amazed at her journey and inspired by her wisdom and depth. She ended with these words: "God's provision in my life enables me—a woman with no hands and feet—to say that I have never been more whole and blessed. He loves me and has given me purpose. He provides hope, a plan, and a future."[4]

Yahweh Yireh Provides His Presence

Cyndi's message is relevant not only to the women in my study but also to you, dear reader. Through Jesus Christ, *Yahweh Yireh* has provided all things necessary for you to flourish. If circumstances unravel around you, remember that God loves you and has created you for a purpose. No matter what challenges you face today, God's provision of his presence will give you strength and courage to persevere and rise above the fray.

Like Cyndi, perhaps you're experiencing a detour you could never have imagined. Without a moment's notice, the path on which you were walking took a sudden turn, and the road you're traveling now is so steep that it leaves you gasping for air and struggling to take the next step.

If you could sit down for coffee with the Old Testament character Joseph and tell him about your experience, he would likely listen with empathy and say, "I understand. Been there, done that."

Joseph was seventeen years old when his brothers betrayed him. Jealous that he was their father's favorite and fed up with his dreams that implied he had authority over them, they sold him to traders who were headed to Egypt (Genesis 37:2-28). There Joseph became a slave in Potiphar's household (Genesis 37:36), where everything surrounding him was unfamiliar: the food, language, customs, and people, including their lavish lifestyle and the gods they worshiped. Only one constant from Joseph's past remained: God's presence.

Joseph's life took another detour after he rejected the advances of Potiphar's wife. Falsely accused of sexual assault, he landed in prison, where shackles bruised his feet and an iron collar encircled his neck (Genesis 39:6-20; Psalm 105:17-18). Yet there, too, God was with him (Genesis 39:21). Scripture doesn't tell us whether Joseph doubted the presence of God, but we know without a doubt that God never abandoned him. Neither does he abandon us. He won't, and he can't. He made a promise to never leave or forsake us, and he can't break it because of who he is:

> God is not a man, so he does not lie.
> He is not human, so he does not change his mind.
> Has he ever spoken and failed to act?
> Has he ever promised and not carried it through?

> NUMBERS 23:19

"Never let the presence of a storm cause you to doubt the presence of God," says Craig Groeschel.[5] We need this reminder, because our human bent always leans toward the negative. When life leads us down the path of suffering, we often doubt God's intent for us. We question his goodness, wisdom, and sovereignty. It's easy to wonder, *Does he truly care about me? Or is he so busy with bigger concerns that my circumstances take a back seat?* Yet because of who he is, *Yahweh Yireh* remains engaged with us and always sees to it that our needs are met. And when we're in a hard place, our greatest need is his presence.

In the Bible, God sometimes revealed his presence in an obvious way, like when he showed up in a cloud by day and a pillar of fire by night to lead the Israelites through the wilderness (Exodus 13:21). His presence, displayed in this way for all to see, gave his people confidence that they were not alone. He was with them to ensure their well-being.

When God's presence appears less obvious, however, does that make it less real? Absolutely not. "We [Christians] are always in the presence of God.... There is never a nonsacred moment! His presence never diminishes. Our awareness of his presence may falter, but the reality of his presence never changes," writes Max Lucado.[6]

I invite you to pause here and take a few minutes to recall times when God has revealed his presence to you in obvious ways. Maybe he showed up in a friend's phone call or email, bearing encouragement when you needed it most. Perhaps you recognized his presence in a stranger's kindness or in the beauty of a sunrise or in a nature walk through a forest. Maybe he showed up in a song, a sermon, or a meaningful quote.

Take a moment to thank *Yahweh Yireh* for gifting you with these precious revelations of his engagement in your life. Thank him that the reality of his presence never changes, even when you experience days that prey on your fears. No doubt Joseph experienced a few days like that, but this we know: God was with him, and he's with us too.

Yahweh Yireh's Ultimate Provision

In this session, I've shared stories of how *Yahweh Yireh* has met my family's material needs, and how we all can take refuge in the provision of his presence. I also shared how Abraham experienced *Yahweh Yireh* at a critical moment of testing, and how Cyndi experienced *Yahweh Yireh* through his provisions of hope, emotional and physical strength, courage, and healing. I mentioned Joseph and how he experienced *Yahweh Yireh*'s presence even in the prison cell.

All of this might sound nicely comprehensive, but we've barely scratched the surface. The beauty and scope of *Yahweh Yireh* cannot be fully understood or appreciated without acknowledging him as the great I AM. He embodies everything for which our souls yearn. In the words of Jennifer Kennedy Dean, "He never creates us with a need that He himself [does not] supply."[7]

> Yahweh Yireh *did the hardest thing ever when he sent Jesus to die in our place.*

The greatest need you and I have is for a relationship with our Creator, and *Yahweh Yireh* met that need through Christ Jesus. Just as he provided the sheep to be slain on Isaac's behalf, so he provided his Son, Jesus—the perfect, spotless Lamb of God—to be slain on our behalf. His death paid the penalty we owe for our sin and set us free from the fear of judgment and eternal death:

> *It was not with perishable things such as silver or gold that you were redeemed from the empty way of life handed down to you from your ancestors, but with the precious blood of Christ, a lamb without blemish or defect. He was chosen before the creation of the world, but was revealed in these last times for your sake.*
>
> 1 PETER 1:18-20 NIV

Everything we need, he is—and more. We lack nothing when he is our everything. As *Yahweh Yireh* in the flesh, Jesus is the bread of life that satisfies our deepest hunger (John 6:32–35). He is the living water that quenches our thirst (John 7:37–39). He is our joy when we feel downcast (John 15:11) and our peace when we feel distressed (Ephesians 2:14). He's our wisdom when we need answers (1 Corinthians 1:30), our guide when we need direction (Psalm 32:8), and our comfort when we need consolation (2 Corinthians 1:3–4).

We stand on a promise the apostle Paul penned to Philippian believers two thousand years ago, because its truth has not changed: "My God will meet all your needs according to the riches of his glory in Christ Jesus" (Philippians 4:19 NIV).

Yahweh Yireh did the hardest thing ever when he sent Jesus to die in our place. If he was willing to go to that extent to see to it that our need for forgiveness and restoration was met, then we can surely trust him to meet all our other needs.

How Shall We Respond?

Yahweh Yireh invites us to tell him our needs. We might wonder if that's a bit redundant since, after all, he already knows about them, right?

Yes, he does. Our needs are no surprise to our all-knowing heavenly Father, but he wants us to express those needs to him anyway, because he values engagement with us. He truly cares.

First, let's choose not to cave in to fear. Our confidence in the Lord comes from knowing that he cherishes us and has our best interests in mind. We can trust him and not be afraid.

Second, let's bring our requests to God. The apostle Paul's instructions to the believers in Philippi contain wise counsel for us when we experience a need: "Do not be anxious about anything, but in every situation, by prayer and petition, with thanksgiving, present your requests to God" (Philippians 4:6–7 NIV).

Depending on the nature of the need, I've often prayed, "Provide in a way for which there is no human explanation." Scripture tells us that he's able to do "immeasurably more than all we ask or imagine" (Ephesians 3:20 NIV), so why not invite him to show up and show off? Why not ask him to meet our needs in a way that leaves onlookers in awe of who he is? Ask for a God story that gives him glory.

Third, let's have the correct attitude and mindset when we present those needs. When we ask God to provide for a specific need, let's be sure to ask according to his will as revealed in Scripture.

For instance, say you're in the market to buy a home. Asking God to bless you with a winning lottery ticket so that you can buy a house you can't afford isn't the way to go. Instead, ask him to guide you to the house he has already chosen for you.

Or perhaps you need guidance in making a major decision. Asking him for direction and then turning to a horoscope or an astrologer isn't God's way of doing things. Instead, read the Word, ask godly friends to pray, and wait for God to work on your behalf.

When we express our needs to *Yahweh Yireh*, let's be mindful that we might see an immediate response to our prayers—but not always. If that's the case, let's resist the temptation to run ahead of him. Let's trust his sovereignty and power. Remember: His timing is impeccable, and his wisdom is far beyond ours.

God doesn't need our help to provide for us, but he often gives us a role to play in our needs being met. For example, he's capable of miraculously dropping a job in our laps, but generally it's our responsibility to look for work and fill out job applications. Taking initiative is our role, and providing us with work is his.

Fourth, let's replace a sense of entitlement with a heart of gratitude for everything he has already provided in the past. And while we're talking to *Yahweh Yireh* about our needs, let's say thank-you in advance for what he will do in the future.

This is not being presumptuous. Rather, it's living from the truth that God is good by nature and does only good on our behalf. Whatever his response to our expressed needs, we can be confident that it will be good, even if it looks different than what we wish.

One thing is for sure—*Yahweh Yireh* provides for us because that's who he is. And when he provides, it is always enough. In his care, we lack no good thing.

Prayer

Yahweh Yireh, I praise you for being all-knowing. I can rest assured that you know my needs before I express them—and that you know the best means for meeting them. Thank you especially for providing Jesus as the perfect sacrifice to die in my place, meeting my greatest need. I am eternally grateful. Thank you for giving me everything I need to flourish and for fulfilling my needs so generously. Because of who you are, I am free from fearing any kind of lack. Help me walk in the truth of this manifestation of your character, and transform me through the process. In Jesus's name, amen.

Points TO *Ponder*

1 **Read 2 Corinthians 9:8 in the ESV Bible version.**

- What word is mentioned four times?

- What does this word reveal about God's character?

- How have you experienced God's grace and sufficiency in fulfilling a task he's given you?

2 **Read Romans 8:32 in the ESV.**

- God did the most difficult thing ever for us when we least deserved it. What does that say about his willingness to provide anything we need to flourish?

- What is his attitude when he provides for us?

- How does this encourage you to trust *Yahweh Yireh* to meet your needs?

3 Read Psalm 84:11.

■ What provisions are mentioned in this verse?

■ What condition accompanies them?

■ What does this infer about our responsibility when we ask God to meet our needs?

4 Read John 14:27.

■ Jesus knew his disciples would face fear-filled days, so he provided them with a gift. What was that gift?

■ How have you experienced this gift when you've faced a frightening situation?

 **Read John 14:1-3.**

- What divine provision is mentioned?

- How does this encourage you considering the uncertainties you face?

Scan the QR code or go to

**hendricksonrose.org/
LivingUnafraidSession4**

for more author insights about
the name *Yahweh Yireh*.

SESSION 5

Yahweh Tzevaot

The LORD of Hosts

THE *SNAP CAME FIRST.* Excruciating pain followed a nanosecond later. I yelped for help and limped to a bench three steps away. An immediate trip to the emergency room confirmed my suspicions: I'd suffered a ruptured Achilles tendon.

Unfortunately, the injury came as no surprise. Too much comfort food, too many hours sitting at my desk, and too little exercise had left me stiff and in chronic pain for several years. My body was a wreck, and a battle to recover my health had to begin.

First, I fought the challenges that came with moving about our three-story townhouse while wearing a non–weight-bearing cast. The battle intensified a week later when an injury on the opposite leg landed me in a wheelchair. Then came knee surgery and twice-weekly physical therapy appointments.

But wait—there's more.

Full-blown menopause and insomnia struck. Exhaustion swept over me every afternoon like a tsunami that sucked my energy out to sea and left me floundering to hold a coherent conversation. Then my body cried, "Enough!" and shingles broke out.

In the middle of my crises came our ministry's annual staff conference in Romania. I couldn't attend for obvious reasons, but I encouraged Gene to go. He hesitated, so I put on my brave face and insisted, "Don't worry about me. I'll be fine." What was I thinking?

I hit a physical and emotional wall six days after Gene left. When morning dawned after yet another sleepless night, I muttered the only prayer I could muster: "Jesus, help!" I grabbed my Bible and flipped to Psalms for a word, a phrase, a promise—anything to provide a knot at the end of my rope. My eyes landed on these words from Psalm 74:4: "You don't let me sleep."

How appropriate, I thought.

"I am too distressed even to pray!"

Me too.

The psalmist's continued lament described my feelings, and his rapid-fire questions mirrored mine:

> *I think of the good old days,*
> > *long since ended,*
> *when my nights were filled with joyful songs.*
> > *I search my soul and ponder the difference now.*
> *Has the Lord rejected me forever?*
> > *Will he never again be kind to me?*
> *Is his unfailing love gone forever?*
> > *Have his promises permanently failed?*
> *Has God forgotten to be gracious?*
> > *Has he slammed the door on his compassion?*

> > > > PSALM 77:5–9

But then his focus and tone changed:

> *When the Red Sea saw you, O God,*
> > *its waters looked and trembled!*
> > *The sea quaked to its very depths.*
> *Your road led through the sea,*
> > *your pathway through the mighty waters—*
> > *a pathway no one knew was there!*
> *You led your people along that road like a flock of sheep,*
> > *with Moses and Aaron as their shepherds.*

> > > PSALM 77:16, 19–20

I envisioned my broken health and limited mobility spread like the Red Sea before me. I stood and gazed longingly at wellness on the far shore as my enemies—self-condemnation, discouragement, and fear—threatened to overtake me.

You'll never fully recover, an inner voice taunted. *You did this to yourself, and you lack the self-discipline to turn things around. Regaining your health is impossible. This is your new normal, so get used to it.*

But just as the psalmist's perspective had shifted, something began to shift in my thinking. I envisioned that my current circumstances were trembling in God's presence. I imagined him going to battle on my behalf and creating a path through my Red Sea. I felt empowered to follow his lead, trusting him to help me fight the enemy of despair and deliver me safely on the opposite shore.

Maybe you can relate to my battle with obesity, injuries, and chronic pain, and the subsequent feelings of helplessness and discouragement. Or perhaps you struggle with an addiction, a need for control, an eating disorder, or perfectionism.

> *If we attempt to battle spiritual forces in our own strength, there is no way we can win.*

Maybe you're wrestling with a difficult relationship. I know how it feels to be criticized, misunderstood, and falsely accused—all based on wrong assumptions. I've struggled through hurt, anger, and unforgiveness more times than I care to count.

Perhaps your mind is a battleground where warring thoughts rage. You strive to focus on all things lovely and true, but thoughts of the opposite nature consistently push their way into your mental space. Or maybe worry and fear join forces to defeat the calm and peace your soul craves.

We're all engaged in battles of a spiritual nature, "for we are not fighting against flesh-and-blood enemies, but against evil rulers and authorities of the unseen world, against mighty powers in this dark world, and against evil spirits in the heavenly places" (Ephesians 6:12). And if we attempt to battle spiritual forces in our own strength, there is no way we can win.

That's why we need God to fight for us. There's no one stronger, more trustworthy, and more capable than *Yahweh Tzevaot*.

Yahweh Tzevaot: What Does It Mean?

The Hebrew word *tzevaot* (pronounced "tzeh-vah-OAT") means "hosts" or "armies" and implies the amassing of forces, sometimes within a military context. Combined with *Yahweh*, it means "The LORD of Hosts." This has three possible applications from Scripture:

1. God is commander in chief of the armies of men.

   The sound of a tumult is on the mountains as of a great multitude! The sound of an uproar of kingdoms, of nations gathering together! The LORD of hosts is mustering a host for battle.

   ISAIAH 13:4 ESV

2. God is chief over angelic beings, both good and evil.

   Micaiah said, "Therefore hear the word of the LORD: I saw the LORD sitting on his throne, and all the host of heaven standing beside him on his right hand and on his left."

   1 KINGS 22:19 ESV

3. God is supreme over all the heavenly hosts—sun, moon, stars, and planets.

   By the word of the LORD the heavens were made, and by the breath of his mouth all their host.

   PSALM 33:6 ESV

Theologians agree on these possible applications, and they also agree that we needn't choose one over the other, since God is God over all.

Different Bible versions translate this name in different ways. For instance, the New International Version says "The LORD Almighty," and the New Living Translation, "The LORD of Heaven's Armies." The New American Standard Bible uses "The LORD of armies," and the English Standard Version, "The LORD of hosts."

No matter how biblical scholars translate it, the name *Yahweh Tzevaot* reminds us of God's authority and power over everything. *E-v-e-r-y-t-h-i-n-g.* Nothing visible or invisible exists over which *Yahweh Tzevaot* does not rule. Nothing stands against him. Because of who he is—commander and mighty warrior—nothing stands in his way. He accomplishes the victory for those who trust in him.

Yahweh Tzevaot occurs for the first time in 1 Samuel 1:3. A man named Elkanah traveled annually to Shiloh—where the Ark of the Covenant was kept in the tabernacle before the temple was built—"to worship and sacrifice to the LORD of Heaven's Armies."

Perhaps the writer used this name for God to differentiate the focus of Elkanah's worship from the pagan religions of the surrounding nations. They worshiped the sun, moon, and stars, but Elkanah worshiped the one who created and ruled over those heavenly bodies.

Yahweh Tzevaot is mentioned next when Elkanah's wife Hannah used this name in her prayer. Let's take a deep dive to see what we can learn from her life, shall we?

Hannah Discovers God as *Yahweh Tzevaot*

As a woman unable to conceive, Hannah found life anything but easy. She lived in a society that considered infertility a tragedy and a sign of God's displeasure. She was likely rejected by others and mocked in the marketplace, but the worst ridicule came from within the walls of her own home.

Hannah's husband, Elkanah, loved her deeply, but he had a second wife, Peninnah, and that led to trouble. Peninnah had children but desired love. Hannah had love but desired children. Thus began a rivalry that Scripture describes in this way: "[Hannah's] rival used to provoke her grievously to irritate her, because the LORD had closed her womb. So it went on year by year" (1 Samuel 1:6–7 ESV).

The emotional pain of infertility and Peninnah's abuse took a toll on Hannah. Sadness overwhelmed her. She wept bitterly and lost her appetite. She grew irritable and suffered great distress.

Perhaps her sorrow was worsened by the fear of not having a child to care for her in her old age and the fear of her husband's love growing cold if she didn't conceive. A study about infertility in the Old Testament says that Hannah's story contains sufficient evidence to make a diagnosis of depression probable.[1]

Hannah faced a battle on a second front when, sadly, Elkanah added to her sorrow. He was loving but a little clueless. He could not understand his wife's longing for a child, so he peppered her with questions like, "Hannah, why do you weep? And why do you not eat? And why is your heart sad?" And the clincher: "Am I not more to you than ten sons?" (1 Samuel 1:8 ESV).

On one of their visits to Shiloh, Hannah went to the tabernacle to pray. Here, for the first time in Scripture, we see the name *Yahweh Tzevaot* used in prayer: "O LORD of hosts, if you will indeed look on the affliction of your servant and remember me and not forget your servant, but will give to your servant a son, then I will give him to the LORD all the days of his life, and no razor shall touch his head" (1 Samuel 1:11 ESV).

Hannah meant business. Calling on *Yahweh Tzevaot* for help acknowledged his authority over all things, including her womb and Elkanah's second wife. It acknowledged his power to fight the two-front battle on her behalf, and it resulted in a peace she hadn't known for a long, long time.

Eli, the priest in the tabernacle, had observed Hannah's lips moving as she prayed. But because she was praying in her heart and not with her voice, Eli assumed she was drunk. Hannah could have burst into tears over his accusation or blasted him for assuming the worst, but she did not. Instead, she responded with respect as she explained her situation. Eli then blessed her, and Hannah left with a transformed countenance and a restored appetite (1 Samuel 1:12–18).

In his book *Perfect Trust*, Pastor Chuck Swindoll exhorts, "Walk by faith! Stop this plagued biting of nails and weariness of worry that you encourage within when the tests come. Relax! Learn to say, 'Lord, this is Your battle.'"[2]

That's exactly what Hannah did. She walked by faith in *Yahweh Tzevaot* and stopped the plague of worry about what her future held if it never held a baby. She chose to relax and rest in God's power and authority. She surrendered her battle to the one who commands every army, seen and unseen. In turn, he changed her perspective and set her free. He also answered her prayer. Within a year, Hannah delivered a son and named him Samuel.

> **The Lord of Hosts *is never too busy to lean down and listen to our distraught cries.***

You might read Hannah's story and think, *Well, that's good for Hannah, but I'm not her. My situation is different.* That is true. But let's remember that she was just an ordinary person, brokenhearted over hurtful issues and difficult relationships.

Sound familiar? Like Hannah, we're ordinary people too. And we're often brokenhearted over hurtful issues and difficult relationships. But also like Hannah, we don't have to stay stuck in that place. We, too, can call on *Yahweh Tzevaot* and pour out our pain to him. He's *The Lord of Hosts*, but he's never too busy to lean down and listen to our distraught cries.

Deb's Story: When Victory Looks Different

One of my grandkids' favorite bedtime books is *Ten Little Night Stars*, by Deb Gruelle, who is a gifted children's author and a dear friend. No one reading her delightful stories would ever guess she's a modern-day Hannah who has prayed in anguish to *Yahweh Tzevaot*.

Deb and her husband lived in married-student housing while attending seminary. But while most of the other young couples there got pregnant, the Gruelles struggled with infertility.

Deb had grown up in a Christian home, served as a leader in her youth group, and participated in Bible studies. She figured that if she made good choices, she could count on God to bless her life. When efforts to start a family failed repeatedly, she wondered why God was denying her.

"I couldn't imagine going on without having children," said Deb. "Being a mother was a calling I feared I might never fulfill, so I prayed in anguish. I clung to Hannah's prayer year after year, and I learned through my pain that *The Lord Almighty* hears the cries of anguished women."

Eight years after they married, Deb and her husband had a son. As ten more years passed, they suffered seven miscarriages and five failed adoptions. But Deb kept on praying, and at long last, they welcomed an adopted daughter. Their second son was born three months later.

Deb's battle with infertility was long and painful, but that chapter in her story had a happy ending like Hannah's. Each woman prayed and trusted *Yahweh Tzevaot* to fight her battle, and each experienced a victory with a ripple effect reaching far beyond her home: Hannah's son became a prophet and the last (and perhaps greatest) of Israel's judges; Deb wrote *Aching for a Child*, a book to educate and encourage couples struggling with infertility. Twenty years later, a publisher in Hungary released it with updates to ensure its relevance in that culture. The book, which also addresses the impact of pornography on a couple's relationship, has had far-reaching influence in a country historically considered a porn giant.

Yahweh Tzevaot brought a joyous conclusion to Hannah's and Deb's similar battles so that their heart's desire was satisfied. We might assume, then, that he will come through for us in the same way, even if it takes longer than we like. We only need to hang in there until it happens.

Such a train of thought proves true in some situations, but let's remember this: Yes, *Yahweh Tzevaot* can win our battles, whatever their nature, because he is powerful. But because he is also wise and good, he sometimes fights on our behalf to accomplish a victory that looks different from the one we are wishing for.

It's easy to celebrate when God rallies the forces and accomplishes what looks and feels to us like a true win—for instance, when he provides a well-paying job, restores a faltering marriage, brings the prodigal home, or heals our hurting bodies. But what about when his idea of a victory seems to fall short of our idea?

When this happens—and it will—our role is to trust the commander in chief. His understanding is far superior to ours because his perspective is far greater. His idea of a true win involves growing deeper in our relationship with him, becoming more like Jesus, and bearing spiritual fruit. In contrast, our concept involves getting our prayers answered the way we want and our problems solved as soon as possible.

But "sometimes God will allow you to experience larger problems in life because He wants to unveil a larger portion of Himself to you," says Tony Evans. "People who want to give up on God simply because life's scenarios don't make sense could very well be walking away from a new manifestation of God and His name in their lives."[3]

Deb refused to give up trusting in God for a family, and as a result, she discovered that *Yahweh Tzevaot* hears the prayers of an anguished woman.

And then he allowed her to experience a larger problem in life: When Deb's kids were three, four, and thirteen, she developed a chronic disease called myalgic encephalomyelitis.

Deb suffered from extreme fatigue, pain throughout her body, and memory loss. Communication also became difficult: She stuttered, slurred her words, and struggled with aphasia—the loss of the ability to express and understand speech.

Deb lost her ability to walk and drive, and for a period of about ten years, she was barely able to leave her house. On rare occasions when she was able to attend church, she had to lie on a pew in the back because sitting for an hour was too difficult.

Deb saw a multitude of doctors and spent thousands on medicines and supplements, and she and many others, including her church elders, also prayed for healing. She believed that *Yahweh Tzevaot* could win this war with a single word, but it appeared he was choosing not to.

As Deb fought this battle for her health, her marriage ended in divorce. Her world had shrunk, and her body had become a prison. Parenting two teenagers and facing the need to move to a different state, she feared she wouldn't be able to survive on her own. At times she wondered if God had placed her on a shelf, and now she'd reached her expiration date. Yet she clung to him because she believed life wasn't worth living apart from him.

Some of Deb's symptoms have disappeared or lessened over time, but she still walks with a cane and deals daily with physical and cognitive limitations. From our human perspective, we might label Deb's situation a lost battle; from a heavenly perspective, however, this is a battle won: Deb's suffering has fostered compassion for others living with chronic and invisible illnesses. It has deepened her relationship with God and borne fruit—despite her limitations, Deb has written several books that have blessed hundreds of thousands of children, my grandchildren included. *This* is a victory.

"I don't know how I'll survive in the future," said Deb, "but I know God loves me and has my best interest at heart. That truth, combined with knowing he is all-powerful, frees me to live from a sense of security and inner rest."

When fearful thoughts occasionally appear, Deb battles them by recalling *Yahweh Tzevaot*'s strength and faithfulness during past difficult times. She reminds herself that she needn't worry, because he is mighty to save her from whatever problems she faces—whether small or catastrophic. She chooses to trust that he'll come through for her. What that looks like, no one knows. But Deb knows this: God loves her.

"We call on *The Lord of Heaven's Armies* to surround and protect us in the battles of life," she remarked. "Sometimes he doesn't answer our deepest prayers as we hope, but he still loves us. The miracle is that he is with us, protecting and sustaining and providing for us amid the battles that rage around us."[4]

Jesus as *Yahweh Tzevaot*

As we've learned, God knows that it is difficult for us to trust an invisible God without a true understanding of who he is, so in his love he not only manifests himself to us through his names but also through Jesus. Because Jesus is God incarnate, he is *Yahweh Tzevaot* in the flesh—the one who can protect, sustain, and provide throughout a raging battle.

Isaiah referred to Jesus by this name when he prophesied his coming: "Our Redeemer, whose name is the LORD of Heaven's Armies [*Yahweh Tzevaot*], is the Holy One of Israel" (Isaiah 47:4). And as Jesus told his disciples, "Anyone who has seen me has seen the Father!" (John 14:9). Trusting an invisible God to carry us through life's tough stuff becomes a lot easier when we realize the scope of his power as revealed through Jesus. Prepare to be amazed!

For starters, Jesus raised the dead, restored sight to the blind, and healed the lame and lepers (Matthew 11:4–6). He demonstrated authority over the forces of nature by walking on water and calming a wild windstorm (Matthew 14:25; Mark 4:35–41), and as he hung on the cross, daylight turned to darkness for three hours (Luke 23:44).

Jesus also demonstrated power over evil hosts. Demons shrieked in terror and begged for mercy in his presence. On one occasion, a demon inside a man identified himself by the name Legion (Mark 5:1–20; Luke 8:26–39). The word *legion* commonly referred to a Roman troop of up to 6,000 men, so it's possible that 6,000 demons possessed the man. Yet Jesus cast them out with a mere verbal command!

On the night he was arrested, Jesus gave a glimpse of his might as *Yahweh Tzevaot*. Peter, one of his disciples, attempted to protect him by brandishing his sword and slicing off the ear of the high priest's servant. Jesus responded by healing the man. "Do you think that I cannot appeal to my Father, and he will at once send me more than twelve legions of angels?" Jesus asked (Matthew 26:53 ESV).

Let's do the math. If one legion represents as many as 6,000 angels, and we multiply that by 12, we now have approximately 72,000 angelic heavenly hosts. But Jesus implied even more than that were standing ready to aid him. That's mind-boggling, but there's more.

Isaiah tells us that the angel of the LORD killed 185,000 Assyrian soldiers in one night (Isaiah 37:33–36). Because of the phrase used ("the angel of the LORD" instead of the less specific "an angel"), theologians believe this event was a theophany—an appearance of God, perhaps Jesus himself, in the Old Testament.

But also consider this: If every angel possessed anything close to this level of strength, twelve legions of angels could take out *a lot* of warriors. It's almost comical that Peter believed Jesus needed his protection and could save him with a sword wielded by a mere human. I can only imagine Jesus shaking his head and saying to Peter, "Son, put that thing away."

What do you believe, my friend? Though he is invisible, can we trust *Yahweh Tzevaot* to protect, sustain, and provide for us amid life's raging battles? Can we accept his invitation to cast our cares on him? Is he big enough to handle those larger problems that he allows us to experience?

Our finite minds cannot grasp God's infinite strength at work on our behalf. Nor can we grasp his grace. When we come to him with desperate prayers and broken hearts, *Yahweh Tzevaot* stoops to listen, and then he battles on our behalf. Now we can say,

> Goodbye, fear. Hello, freedom.
> Goodbye, anxiety. Hello, anticipation.
> Goodbye, worry. Hello, wonder.

Understanding the depth and scope of this spiritual reality forever changes us.

Yahweh Tzevaot Defeats Our Giants

I grew up on a diet of Bible stories, including the account of David and Goliath. This classic tale of little guy versus big bully has always been a personal favorite—because the little guy wins.

David was a teenage shepherd overlooked by others and scorned by his brothers, but God noticed him and manifested a larger portion of himself to the boy. This revelation came when lions and bears tried to devour the sheep in David's care. Rather than seek his own safety, David ran after the predators and snatched the sheep from their mouths. If the beasts turned on him, he killed them with his bare hands. David knew he didn't accomplish this feat in his own strength and credited God with the victory (1 Samuel 17:34-37).

One day, David went to see his three oldest brothers while they were serving in the Israelite army. The army was engaged in battle with the Philistines, and the Philistine giant Goliath had shown up twice a day for forty days to flaunt himself and taunt the Israelites. The Israelites ran from Goliath in fear, but David ran toward him in faith. He declared,

> *You come to me with a sword and with a spear and with a*
> *javelin, but I come to you in the name of the LORD of hosts*
> *... whom you have defied. This day the LORD will deliver you*
> *into my hand, and I will strike you down.... For the battle is*
> *the LORD's, and he will give you into our hand.*

> 1 SAMUEL 17:45-47 ESV

Like David, we, too, face giants that loom large. We battle with health and financial concerns, difficult relationships, and bad habits we can't kick. We wrestle with hurtful memories we can't erase and harmful behaviors we can't stop. But here's the thing: We, too, can share in David's courage by not letting our giants intimidate or paralyze us with fear.

God revealed his almighty power to David through encounters with wild animals, and David lived by focusing on the truth of that revelation. Experiencing God's might on the "sheep field" gave him courage on the battlefield. In similar fashion, since God has revealed his character to us through his names and through Jesus, let's live out the truth of these revelations.

We don't face our giants with man-made weapons. We don't take them down with the latest self-help strategies, trendy philosophies, or the world's so-called wisdom. We face them in the name of *The Lord of Heaven's Armies*. Because of who he is, nothing is impossible for him. Nothing, that is, except defeat. Author and speaker Christine Caine says,

> God is faithful. He'll fulfill every promise he's made. There's no disease God cannot heal, no heart he cannot mend, no bondage he cannot break, no enemy he cannot defeat, no mountain he cannot move, and no need he cannot meet. And because that same Spirit lives inside each of us, we move forward undaunted; we are unstoppable; and we live unshakeable. Focus on our unshakeable God instead of the chaos around you and he will carry you through the challenges and on to victory.[5]

No giant can stand in the presence of our unshakeable and undefeatable God. Allowing this spiritual reality to take hold of us can radically transform our lives.

Remember the physical issues I talked about at the beginning of this session? I'd battled with weight issues for years by swinging my little sword of human effort—aka fad diets—but nothing worked. God used the experiences of my injuries, partial mobility loss, insomnia, and shingles to unveil a larger portion of himself to me.

Yes, suffering gave me an opportunity to experience him as *Yahweh Tzevaot*. I cried to *The Lord of Heaven's Armies*, and he led me through my Red Sea on a path that connected me to First Place for Health, a ministry that focuses on wellness in every part of who we are.[6] I joined one of their weekly online Bible studies, where I learned more about nutrition and fitness. I began to track my food and became accountable to the group leader. *Yahweh Tzevaot* gave me the desire and strength to exercise regularly, and he helped me identify and stop believing the lies I'd entertained about never regaining my health.

> **Nothing is impossible for Yahweh Tzevaot. Nothing, that is, except defeat.**

Two years of intentional effort later, I reached the level of recovery a therapist had predicted would be unlikely due to the nature of my injuries. Victory was accomplished because *The Lord of Heaven's Armies* stooped to listen to my cry, and I began to live out the truth of who he is—the one who rescues us and does battle on our behalf.

How Shall We Respond?

Yahweh Tzevaot wants us to know him, not as a mere acquaintance, but as an intimate friend. Imagine: *The Lord of Heaven's Armies* invites us to pour out our hearts to him, give him our deepest pain and greatest challenges, and trust him to battle on our behalf. We can do no less than say yes. Knowing God in this way doesn't just happen; it requires intentional choices and actions on our part. Following are four key actions for developing friendship with God, using the acronym ARMY.

A : **Adore**

When the Old Testament prophet Isaiah had a vision of God, he cried, "Holy, holy, holy is the Lord of Heaven's Armies! The whole earth is filled with his glory!" (Isaiah 6:3). The Hebrew word for *holy* means "separate," and it comes from an ancient word that means "to cut" or "to separate"; that's where we get the expression "a cut above the rest."[7] In essence, Isaiah declared that *Yahweh Tzevaot* is "a cut above the rest," "a cut above the rest," "a cut above the rest." Theologian R. C. Sproul wrote, "He is an infinite cut above everything else."[8] *Yahweh Tzevaot* is so amazing that our minds cannot begin to comprehend his splendor. Pause a moment to think about his excellence and praise him for who he is.

R : Repent

"To repent" means we turn from our own way and return to God's way. We choose to obey his directives, not from duty but from desire. We want to show our love for him by living as he says. The Hebrew prophet Amos said, "Do what is good and run from evil so that you may live! Then the LORD God of Heaven's Armies will be your helper" (Amos 5:14). Confess to God the sins that come to mind, and then receive his forgiveness. Don't let anything stand between you and him. Nothing is worthy of our time, attention, and affection if it hinders friendship with *Yahweh Tzevaot*.

M : Move

Sooner or later, God will lead us into a faith-testing situation. When that happens, let's not run away. Let's slip our hands into his and stay close to him. Let's move forward with him, even when we are afraid, because along the way, we will discover new gems about *The Lord of Heaven's Armies*. The Israelites witnessed God's power as they walked through the Red Sea between walls of standing water. David experienced God's strength when he took his slingshot and cast a stone at Goliath. We, too, will witness wonders when we move in sync with *Yahweh Tzevaot*.

Y : Yearn

Let's yearn to know God. Let's ask him to give us an unquenchable thirst for his Word and a hunger for the power of his Holy Spirit in our lives. Let's be quick to repent from known sin so nothing can hinder our relationship with him. Let's determine to turn to him first when we hit a hard place and to seek him to satisfy the deepest longings of our souls. Let's ask him for further revelations of his character as *Yahweh Tzevaot*. Guaranteed, he will answer our prayers. But be forewarned: The only place we can witness him *do* battle is *in* battle.

Prayer

Yahweh Tzevaot, I praise you for being *The Lord of Hosts*. Because of who you are, I can trust you with all my heart. Keep my focus on you when battles rage around me. Keep my confidence in you alone, because you are faithful and mighty to accomplish the victory. Help me walk in the truth of this manifestation of your character, and transform me through the process. In Jesus's name, amen.

Points TO Ponder

---

1 **Read Isaiah 44:6-8.**

- Identify the name used for *Yahweh Tzevaot* (verse 6).

- How does God describe himself throughout this passage?

- Which of these descriptions resonates with you the most, and why?

- How does knowing God as *Yahweh Tzevaot* help you not be afraid?

2 **Read Psalm 27:1-4.**

- Describe David's outlook as he faced physical enemies.

- What was the basis for his confidence?

- Where did David's focus lie?

- On what do you focus when facing a battle?

- On a scale of 1 to 10 (with 10 being very high), rate your confidence during times of battle.

- What practical actions can you take to keep your focus on *Yahweh Tzevaot* amid hardships?

3 **Read Joshua 24:5-14.**

- List the ways in which God battled on the Israelites' behalf.

- Because of everything he had done for them, what did God ask the Israelites to do?

- Compare this passage with Judges 8:34. What can we do to ensure that we—and future generations—remember what God has accomplished on our behalf?

4 Read Psalm 28:7.

- How is God like a shield for those who love him?

- Fill in the blank: I can trust him with _____ my heart.

- For what are you trusting him to help you?

5 Read Psalm 89:5-11.

- How is *Yahweh Tzevaot* described in these verses?

- How have you experienced his faithfulness? His might?

- Read these verses aloud as an act of worship to God.

Scan the QR code or go to

**hendricksonrose.org/
LivingUnafraidSession5**

for more author insights about
the name *Yahweh Tzevaot*.

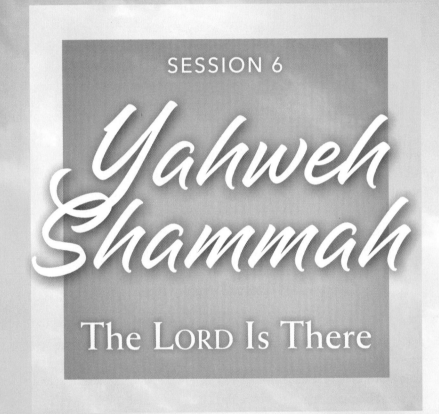

SESSION 6

Yahweh Shammah

The LORD Is There

BREAKFAST HAD JUST begun at a conference I was attending near Budapest, Hungary, when the event host approached me. His expression said it all.

"It's your husband," he remarked as he handed me his phone.

My heart knew what Gene was going to say. For the past three years, my dad's health had slowly declined after he suffered two massive strokes. More than once, Mom had called to tell us that his condition had suddenly worsened and she thought the end was near. But days later, Dad would rally and stabilize until the next sudden turn.

The past couple of weeks, though, had been different. Dad's state had worsened yet again, but this time a comeback seemed unlikely. I flew to Alberta to visit him, and during that time, I faced a most difficult decision: Should I stay with Dad or go on my upcoming trip? Several months earlier, I'd agreed to a speaking tour in Eastern Europe. A conference in Hungary for missionary families was my first scheduled stop, and afterward I planned to stay for two days with Diane, an American coworker living in Slovakia. She would then accompany me by train to fulfill nearly a dozen speaking engagements in Poland and Hungary.

Diane had spent hours coordinating these events and arranging accommodations. I had already purchased my plane ticket to Budapest, prepared my messages, and sent out handouts for translation. The women's ministry leaders in each city had handled advertisements and registrations, pouring their best efforts into the details.

With my departure for Eastern Europe only days away, I sat at Dad's bedside and prayed for wisdom as he slept. Canceling the trip seemed unfair to everyone involved overseas. But what if I made the trip and Dad died before I returned? Not being present to celebrate his life and to support my mom didn't seem right either.

After praying for guidance and discussing my concerns with my family, I sensed God telling me to fulfill my commitment overseas. I said goodbye to my father, returned home to pack my suitcase, and cried all the way to the airport. Twelve hours after I landed in Budapest, my dad took his last breath, and Gene phoned to break the sad news.

My worst fears had come true: Dad was gone, and my mother, siblings, husband, and children would celebrate his life without me. I felt strangely alone in a surreal situation. In retrospect, I don't even know how I managed to keep it together emotionally and mentally. Traveling by train from one city to the next in a foreign country, teaching the Word and praying with women at each event, visiting missionaries in their homes, and sleeping in a different bed every night—all while grieving my father's death—was no small ordeal.

There was only one explanation: *Yahweh Shammah* was with me. His compassion comforted me. His hands carried me. His strength empowered me. His presence made all the difference.

Yahweh Shammah: What Does It Mean?

As painful as my situation was, it provided a precious opportunity to experience God by his name *Yahweh Shammah* (pronounced "SHAHM-mah"), which in Hebrew means "The Lord Is There." It appears only once in the entire Bible: "From that day the name of the city [Jerusalem] will be 'The Lord Is There'" (Ezekiel 48:35).

Ezekiel was a prophet whose messages came at a dark time in Israel's history. The people had rebelled against God—again—and were paying the consequences—again. God allowed the Babylonians to take them into captivity, so now the Israelites were living as strangers in a foreign land. During this time, the Babylonians also destroyed their capital city, Jerusalem, and the holy temple King Solomon had built. The prospect of returning to their homeland waned as time passed, and they lost hope for a better future.

Amid the Israelites' desperation, God spoke through Ezekiel to promise them a future far better than anything they could imagine: Their nation would be restored, and God's presence would dwell among them. To fully appreciate the significance of this message, we must understand that Ezekiel's initial prophecies focused on God's judgment for the Israelites' sin. One of those judgments was the reluctant departure of God's glory from the temple, as described in a vision Ezekiel received (Ezekiel 10:4, 18–19; 11:22–23).

Throughout the generations, God's people had seen his presence manifest in many ways. They had witnessed his power when he rescued them from Egypt (Deuteronomy 4:37). He led them through the wilderness with a cloud and a pillar of fire (Exodus 13:21). When the tabernacle was finished, his presence immediately filled it (Exodus 40:33–38). When Solomon built the temple and offered a dedication prayer, God's presence filled the place so gloriously that the priests could not enter (2 Chronicles 7:1–3).

Time and again, the Israelites beheld God's presence in their midst, but they still turned their backs on him. God sent prophets like Ezekiel to warn them of the consequences if they continued in their rebellion. When they refused to listen, God finally said, "Enough is enough," and he removed his presence. But because God is who he is, he refused to break his covenant of love with them.

The book of Ezekiel is a heavy read, but it ends on a hope-filled note when God promises that his presence will return—*Yahweh Shammah*, "The Lord Is There." The name is referencing Jerusalem, but it reveals an important aspect of God's character: He wanted to assure the Israelites that, although he was allowing them to suffer for a time as a means of discipline, he would not ultimately cast them aside; he would once again dwell with them.

Yahweh Shammah in the Valleys

The name *Yahweh Shammah* gave hope to the Israelites in what felt like a hopeless situation brought on by their own doing. When my dad passed away, I, too, needed reassurance of God's presence—but not because I'd turned my back on him. On the contrary, I'd done what I believed to be right in his eyes. In the painful aftermath, my soul longed to know his nearness in the valley of shadows.

God understood and granted my desire. Within our mission organization, my traveling companion, Diane, was tasked with providing staff care and encouragement. I couldn't spend the next two weeks with a better-equipped person, right? Upon hearing of my dad's passing, she boarded a train to Budapest and came to retrieve me. Her in-home hospitality for the next two days brought a healing balm to my hurting heart.

The morning after I arrived at Diane's, I rose early to read the Word and to journal. A gentle knock on my bedroom door distracted me, and Diane entered with her Bible. "I feel compelled to give you these verses today," she said. Then she read Jesus's words from Luke 14:26–27: "If you want to be my disciple, you must, by comparison, hate everyone else—your father and mother, wife and children, brothers and sisters—yes, even your own life. Otherwise, you cannot be my disciple. And if you do not carry your own cross and follow me, you cannot be my disciple."

Would you give those verses to someone mourning the loss of a loved one? I wouldn't. There's a reason you never see them inside a sympathy card. In this case, however, they hit the target. I needed confirmation that choosing to fulfill my commitment was the right thing to do. I needed to know that I hadn't pursued this speaking tour from selfish motives, that I hadn't somehow left God behind when I crossed the Atlantic Ocean. I needed something ... anything ... that would guard my mind from regrets and second-guesses.

Jesus's words in the Gospel of Luke affirmed me. It's not that I didn't love my father or my family enough to stay home; it's that I loved my Savior enough to go. He had asked me to pick up my cross—the circumstances that called me to die to self-interest—and I'd obeyed, even though it led to a sad and lonely place (Matthew 16:24–26).

As I crawled into bed that evening, my eyes fell on a little devotional book on the nightstand. I flipped to the entry for March 4, the day my father graduated to heaven, and I gasped. The theme verse was the same Scripture Diane had read to me in the morning. What are the chances?

I'll remember that moment as long as I live. God's presence wrapped me up and warmed me from the inside out. I felt lonely, yes, but I wasn't alone. *Yahweh Shammah* was with me. He erased all doubt by loving me through Diane's kindness and affirming me through his Word.

Encountering *Yahweh Shammah* in those difficult circumstances comforted me and strengthened me to do what he'd called me to. He saw me through that surreal time of ministry mingled with mourning, and women's lives were changed for eternity. Mine included.

"God is always with you, even in the darkest night or in the deepest pit," writes poet and philosopher Gift Gugu Mona. "You just need to hold on. Never doubt His presence or power. He will see you through."[1] It's true—God is with us, and we never need to doubt his presence when we're walking in right relationship with him. Even so, we sometimes quickly forget the reality of his presence in the dark, sad, lonely, and un-understandable places of life.

Make no mistake: Satan, the enemy of our souls, will do everything in his power to further our forgetfulness. He begins by messing with our minds, using questions like, *Where was God when _____ happened?* and thoughts like, *You're all alone. No one cares what's happening. Not even God.* Satan tries to convince us that God doesn't even exist and that thinking otherwise puts us out of touch with reality.

Let's not waste precious energy trying to reason with him or make sense of his lies. He's not worth it. Instead, let's fight him with the truths in God's Word, as Jesus did when he faced Satan alone in the wilderness (Matthew 4:1-11).

The Bible is rich with reminders of God's presence. I suggest writing down your favorite Scripture passages and posting them where you'll see them often—on your fridge or bathroom mirror, or beside your kitchen sink or computer monitor. Tuck them in your purse so you can read them on the go. Use them as text for your screen saver. Memorize them so you can meditate on God's truth when the enemy disrupts your sleep. When fear rears its head, pick up these promises and wield them like a sword. Here are five of my favorites:

Don't be afraid, for I am with you. Don't be discouraged, for I am your God. I will strengthen you and help you. I will hold you up with my victorious right hand.

ISAIAH 41:10

The LORD hears his people when they call to him for help. He rescues them from all their troubles. The LORD is close to the brokenhearted; he rescues those whose spirits are crushed.

PSALM 34:17–18

I am convinced that nothing can ever separate us from God's love. Neither death nor life, neither angels nor demons, neither our fears for today nor our worries about tomorrow—not even the powers of hell can separate us from God's love. No power in the sky above or in the earth below— indeed, nothing in all creation will ever be able to separate us from the love of God that is revealed in Christ Jesus our Lord.

ROMANS 8:38–39

Even when I walk through the darkest valley, I will not be afraid, for you are close beside me. Your rod and your staff protect and comfort me.

PSALM 23:4

The LORD your God is living among you. He is a mighty savior. He will take delight in you with gladness. With his love, he will calm all your fears. He will rejoice over you with joyful songs.

ZEPHANIAH 3:17

Yahweh Shammah in Prison and Praises

There's another action you can take to send the enemy on the run when you're in a sad, lonely, I-don't-want-to-be-here place: Practice praise.

The apostle Paul and his coworker Silas had cast out a demon that empowered a slave girl to foretell the future, and afterward her owners' wallets took a hit. Paul and Silas had done nothing wrong, but the slave girl's masters had a different perspective. They dragged Paul and Silas before the authorities, who ordered them beaten with wooden rods and placed in stocks in the inner dungeon of a prison (Acts 16:16–24).

Exercising prayer and praise doesn't necessarily change our circumstances, but it changes us amid those circumstances.

One can only imagine the heat and stench in that dark and windowless prison cell. No one would have blamed Paul and Silas for feeling beaten up, not only physically, but emotionally, mentally, and spiritually as well. No one would have silenced them for bemoaning their circumstances and disgusting surroundings. No one would have shushed them for asking, "Where are you now, God?" But Paul and Silas did none of these things. Instead, they chose to pray and sing praises to God, who, judging by all appearances, had forsaken them (verse 25).

Appearances are deceiving. The two-man worship service began at midnight, and God showed up big-time. "Suddenly, there was a massive earthquake, and the prison was shaken to its foundations. All the doors immediately flew open, and the chains of every prisoner fell off!" (verse 26). When the jailer saw what happened, he and his entire household became Jesus-followers that very night (verse 34). How incredible is that?

Panic is a typical response when we unexpectedly land in a dank, dismal place. Darkness surrounds us, and we forget God's promise to be "our refuge and strength, an ever-present help in trouble" (Psalm 46:1 NIV). Thoughts of abandonment fill our minds, and before long we may feel like a sailor who has fallen overboard unnoticed and is left floundering at sea in the boat's wake (my worst nightmare).

Prayer and praise are atypical when we're in that I-don't-want-to-be-here place. Choosing them over panic demonstrates a determination to trust God, even when we don't understand what's happening around us. It says we expect *Yahweh Shammah* to live up to his name and be fully present with us in that situation. It believes and finds courage in promises like Deuteronomy 31:8: "Do not be afraid or discouraged, for the LORD will personally go ahead of you. He will be with you; he will neither fail you nor abandon you."

Exercising prayer and praise doesn't necessarily change our circumstances, but it changes *us* amid those circumstances. "That's the nature of praise," wrote evangelist Terry Law, who suffered several profound losses in his life. "It draws our attention away from our problems, no matter how overwhelming they are, and lifts our gaze to God."[2]

Paul and Silas lifted their gaze to God in prison and, in their case, experienced his presence in a literal, profound way. Their example sets a high bar, but don't even go near the comparison trap by elevating them to sainthood. Remember, they were ordinary people like you and me. They drew their strength not from within but from the extraordinary God who sat in the cell with them.

This same God, *Yahweh Shammah*, sits with us in our suffering and walks with us through the shadowy valleys. Two thousand years later, he is still present. He is still powerful. He still listens to our prayers. And he is forever worthy of our praise.

Dawn's Story: *Yahweh Shammah* amid Betrayal

Dawn, the executive pastor of a megachurch, decided to purchase a one-way airline ticket from her hometown in Michigan to New Orleans, where her husband was using his construction skills to help residents rebuild following Hurricane Katrina.

Initially, he'd flown back and forth between work and home on weekends, but his visits grew sporadic over time due to the expense. Finally, after an extended absence, he said he would drive home for a short stay. Thinking her husband would appreciate not having to drive from Louisiana to Michigan alone, Dawn arranged her flight as a surprise. Sadly, she was the one who was surprised when she discovered that he was living with another woman. Dawn's husband flew into a rage, forcing her into his truck and then depositing her at a motel.

"It was a long night," said Dawn. "There I sat for twelve hours, weeping profusely. I was dumbfounded, afraid, and feeling completely abandoned. We'd been married twenty-eight years. We had three kids and two grandchildren. I was an executive pastor, and he was a church elder. I knew what this would mean."

Even though Dawn had been the spouse betrayed, she suspected that her failed marriage would cause many within her local Christian community to view her as a poor example of a spiritual leader. She envisioned losing her job, her livelihood, and her ministry. Fear and uncertainty surrounded her in the darkness, and she asked God a question she'd never asked him before: "Why is this happening to me?"

The Holy Spirit answered, *This is not happening to you. It is happening for you, and I want you to trust me.* Dawn found his words comforting. They reassured her that God was well aware of this event and of several other painful experiences in her marriage. Dawn explained, "It was like he said, 'You don't have to do this anymore. You don't have to absorb any more betrayal or pain or hurt. I am going to rescue you. I will take care of you. I am here with you and for you.'"

In the days and weeks ahead, Dawn experienced God as *Yahweh Shammah* in ways that she calls her "God sightings." The next morning, for instance, she flew to Atlanta to stay with her sister, because the shock and trauma had stripped her of strength to fly a further distance. Unbeknownst to Dawn, her kids had driven all night to meet her upon her arrival. As she stepped off the escalator near baggage claim, Dawn saw her children, her sister, and her brother-in-law—and she collapsed. Their arms, like God's strong arms, caught her and supported her.

While at her sister's home, Dawn was reading her Bible and praying one day when she asked, "Lord, where I am going? What am I going to do? Where are you leading me?" She happened to glance up, and her eyes fell on a street sign nailed to the wall. It read "Providence." Dawn said, "It was like God said, 'Trust my providence. I'm here for you. *Yahweh Shammah* is with you.'"

Dawn's suspicions about others' reactions to her marriage breakdown proved true. Her church, wishing to protect itself from criticism, dismissed her with a generous severance package after she told them what had happened in New Orleans. As she sought God for direction about her future, Dawn received a call from a woman pastor she had coached through a difficult journey. She invited Dawn to assume the role of executive pastor at her church.

Shortly after that, a friend phoned and said, "I had a vision while praying for you. I saw an eagle with a nest. It flew to the north, but it returned to the nest as its home base. I feel like God will provide a nest for you. You will go out from it, but you will always return."

Dawn accepted the executive pastor position, and imagine her surprise when she walked into the church and saw a two-story mural of a nest with an eagle sitting in it. Her friend's dream manifested its meaning when Dawn learned the church had two campuses—a home base and one campus to the north. Her job included ministering once a month at the north campus, but she would always return to home base. Dawn also eventually remarried. Five years after her divorce, God brought her a husband whose heart was perfectly aligned with her passion for ministry.[3]

Maybe you can relate to Dawn Damon's story of betrayal. Someone turned on you and shattered your dreams and hopes or tossed you aside and left you feeling empty and alone. If so, please know that *Yahweh Shammah* "is close to the brokenhearted" (Psalm 34:18).

No matter how dark Dawn's circumstances seemed, she chose to believe that God's goodness and presence surrounded her. As she walked the road toward healing, she found hope in Psalm 27:13: "I am still confident of this: I will see the goodness of Yahweh in the land of the living" (web). One day Dawn slipped a comma between *still* and *confident*, and the verse assumed new meaning for her. Now it read, "I am still, confident of this …" Every time fear or panic threatened to overtake her, the words *I am still* reminded her to pause, to put things in proper perspective, and to commit her fears to *Yahweh Shammah*.

Friend, I don't know what challenges you face today, but I wish I could reach beyond these pages and give you a big hug. I can't do that, but someone far better can. He's with you this very moment, wherever you're reading this book—sitting at home in your favorite chair, sipping coffee at a café, nursing your baby during the night, keeping vigil at a loved one's bedside, sunbathing on a beach, warming yourself by a crackling fire, riding the subway, waiting for your kids' soccer practice to end, or flying at 35,000 feet.

No matter where you are or what you're going through, God is with you because he is *Yahweh Shammah*—"The Lord Is There."

Yahweh Shammah—Past, Present, and Future

I love that the meaning of *Yahweh Shammah*'s name is present tense: "The Lord *Is* There." It's not "The Lord *Was* There," for that could indicate that his presence has gone, and nowhere does the Bible say that God checked out after communing with Adam and Eve in the garden, calling Abraham his friend, speaking on the mountain with Moses, leading the Israelites through the wilderness, dwelling in Solomon's temple, protecting Daniel's buddies in the fiery furnace, or sitting in prison with Paul and Silas and Joseph too.

On the contrary, God showed up for his people in ages past, and he does the same for us today. He is alive and well and with us everywhere we go. "We may ignore, but we can nowhere evade, the presence of God," wrote author and scholar C. S. Lewis. "The world is crowded with Him. He walks everywhere *incognito*. And the *incognito* is not always hard to penetrate. The real labour is to remember, to attend. In fact, to come awake. Still more, to remain awake."[4]

The song lyric that speaks to your heart at precisely the right moment? That's God's presence in disguise. The whispered guidance you hear when facing a major decision? The same. The sunrise is his cheery hello, and the sunset splashed across the sky is his goodnight kiss.

When we look for God's presence, it is unavoidable. King David described it this way: "I can never escape from your Spirit! I can never get away from your presence! If I go up to heaven, you are there; if I go down to the grave, you are there. If I ride the wings of the morning, if I dwell by the farthest oceans, even there your hand will guide me, and your strength will support me" (Psalm 139:7-10).

Thankfully, neither does *Yahweh Shammah* mean "The Lord *Will Be* There," for that would imply he is otherwise occupied and puts our calls for help on hold. It might suggest that he responds to our prayers with, "Be patient, okay? I'll be with you in a minute." Or that he's absent and completely detached from us now but will appear someday in the future to devote himself to us then.

That said, a special day does await when we will experience *Yahweh Shammah* on a level much different from the present. As followers of Jesus, we hold fast to the hope of heaven as our future reality, because we believe that all who place their faith in Jesus for salvation will spend eternity with him there (John 3:16; 14:1-3; Philippians 3:20-21; 2 Peter 3:13). What a day that will be when Revelation 21:3 comes to pass: "I heard a loud shout from the throne, saying, 'Look, God's home is now among his people! He will live with them, and they will be his people. God himself will be with them.'"

I don't profess to be a theologian. Neither do I profess to understand end-time prophecies and their many interpretations. But I'm certain of this: Everything surrounding the end times will work out in the end, and God will make his home among his people in a way that will far surpass our wildest imaginations. Sounds like Ezekiel's prophecy coming true!

> **The Lord Is There** *is there for us when we need him most, because he is a present-tense God.*

In the meantime, we live in the present with its celebrations and sorrows. Some days bring laughter and some bring tears. We pray until our knees wear out, and still the answers don't come. We get into trouble trying to fix people or situations beyond our control. The fear of failure keeps us awake at night. The dread of someone exposing our secret addictions or our secret shame prevents us from developing deep and meaningful relationships. Our insecurities drive a wedge between us and those we love.

These issues and more prove our need for God's ever-present help today. Hour by hour. This very moment. Thank goodness, *The Lord Is There* is there for us when we need him most, because he is a present-tense God.

Yahweh Shammah and Jesus

In Old Testament times, God made himself present in the various ways already mentioned in this session. And as we learned with *Yahweh Tzevaot*, he also seems to have shown up as "the angel of the Lord" to deliver special messages (as when he told Gideon to fight the Midianites in Judges 6:11–14); to defend his people from their enemies (as when he killed 185,000 Assyrian soldiers in one night, 2 Kings 19:35); and to let Hagar—a pregnant, distraught Egyptian servant—know that she mattered (Genesis 16:7–13).

When God deemed the time was right, he showed up in an even more impressive way. He humbled himself, took on human form, and moved into our neighborhood (Philippians 2:5–8). The birth of Jesus, God's Son, fulfilled the prophecy in Isaiah 7:14: "The virgin will conceive a child! She will give birth to a son and will call him Immanuel (which means 'God is with us')." The apostle John wrote, "The Word became human and made his home among us" (John 1:14). The writer of the book of Hebrews said, "The Son radiates God's own glory and expresses the very character of God" (Hebrews 1:3).

God maintained his human presence on earth for thirty-three years. Through Jesus's life and ministry, he revealed his character and taught us how to live. Through Jesus's death, he made a way for our sin-severed relationship with him to be reconciled. Through his resurrection, he provided the way for us to live in the victory and beauty of his presence, both now and forever. "For God in all his fullness was pleased to live in Christ, and through him God reconciled everything to himself. He made peace with everything in heaven and on earth by means of Christ's blood on the cross" (Colossians 1:19–20).

In the Old Testament, God promised to never leave his people. Jesus made the same promise before his departure: "Be sure of this: I am with you always, even to the end of the age" (Matthew 28:20). Father and Son kept their promise by sending the Holy Spirit (John 14:16–17), who resides in all who follow Jesus (1 Corinthians 3:16).

The late clergyman, teacher, and author Thomas Keating said, "We rarely think of the air we breathe, yet it is in us and around us all the time. In similar fashion, the presence of God penetrates us, is all around us, is always embracing us."[5] This is totally amazing, is it not? *Yahweh Shammah* is Jesus, the Word made flesh; Immanuel, "God is with us."

How Shall We Respond?

Three actions come to mind when I think about responding appropriately to the life-altering truth revealed by God's name *Yahweh Shammah*— "The LORD Is There":

1. **Believe in God's presence.** I can't count how often I've prayed, "Father, please be with me today." I wonder if he sits in the heavens and shakes his head, saying, "Grace, Grace, when will you learn to believe my promises?" If you're a Jesus-follower as I am and you've prayed the same request, then together let's commit to changing our prayer to "Father, thank you for being with me today." And let's also live by faith, not emotions. "Don't equate the presence of God with a good mood or a pleasant temperament," says Max Lucado. "God is near whether you are happy or not."[6]

2. **Practice God's presence.** Brother Lawrence was a monk who served as a cook in his monastery in the 1600s. Many today regard him as an authority on living moment by moment in the awareness of God's presence. He wrote, "The most holy and necessary practice in our spiritual life is the presence of God. That means finding constant pleasure in His divine company, speaking humbly and lovingly with Him in all seasons, at every moment, without limiting the conversation in any way."[7] As Brother Lawrence did while scrubbing pots and pans, make mundane tasks an act of worship by talking to *Yahweh Shammah* as to a dear friend. When making a meal, thank him for the gift of good food every day. Thank him for hot-water showers, clean drinking water, and clothes you get to wash, dry, and fold. And when you don't feel like talking to him, simply enjoy silence in his company.

3. **Honor God's presence.** Housing the Holy Spirit is an incredible privilege. Let's ensure he feels welcome by keeping our spiritual house clean, so to speak. When he pinpoints sin, confess it, repent, and make restitution with others if

necessary. Let's allow him to develop his spiritual fruits in us so that we reflect Jesus to others.

God's presence surrounds us and dwells within us. Every moment. Everywhere. It's inescapable because he is *Yahweh Shammah*. Like David said in Psalm 139:6, "Such knowledge is too wonderful for me"!

Prayer

Yahweh Shammah, I praise you for being the ever-present God who will never leave or forsake me. Thank you for being near me when my heart is broken. Thank you for surrounding me, for going before me and behind me. Thank you for holding me close, even when others cast me away. I look forward to the coming day when you will take me to my forever home to live in your presence there. In the meantime, your nearness is all I want. Come and satisfy me with your sweet, powerful, holy presence. Help me walk in the truth of this manifestation of your character, and transform me through the process. In Jesus's name, amen.

Points TO *Ponder*

1 **Read Psalm 46:1-2.**

- God is always near and ready to help us. With that truth in mind, complete this sentence: "Therefore, I will not fear when _____."

2 **Read Psalm 34:7 and Psalm 46:7.**

- Who is here among us?

- How might this truth make a difference when you feel like you're fighting a battle alone?

3 **Read Psalm 73:28.**

■ How did the psalmist describe his nearness to God?

■ What actions can you take to draw near to him?

■ How can you avoid a gradual drift away from him?

4 **Read Galatians 2:20.**

■ Who lives in believers?

■ In light of this truth, what must we do?

5 **Read 2 Corinthians 6:16.**

- ■ How does God's presence in us motivate us to live pure lives?

- ■ How does this influence your goals, priorities, and pretty much everything else about you?

Scan the QR code or go to

hendricksonrose.org/ LivingUnafraidSession6

for more author insights about the name *Yahweh Shammah*.

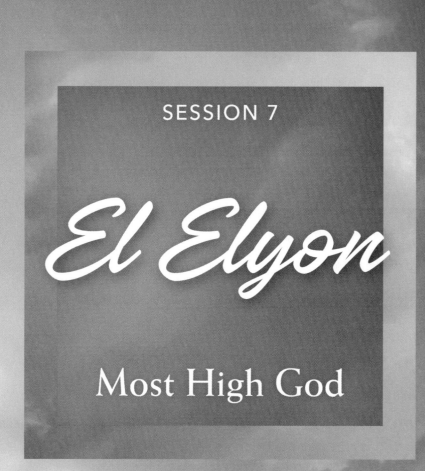

SESSION 7

El Elyon

Most High God

GENE AND I sat at our kitchen table as he listened to me process my feelings aloud. In less than twenty-four hours, I would be embarking on a potentially life-changing path. Rafting down white-water rapids would not have frightened me as much as the challenge ahead of me.

"This is bigger than me," I said, referring to my plan to attend the Florida Christian Writers Conference. I'd never participated in such an event and had no clue what to expect.

The prospect of meeting the editors of my favorite Christian magazines thrilled and intimidated me. The opportunity to learn about writing and publishing intrigued me. But I wouldn't know a soul there—not even the roommate I'd been assigned. The introvert in me tried to hold back her tears but failed.

From the camp where we served on Quadra Island, I would drive alone to Seattle, Washington, and then spend the night in a hotel. The next day I would cross the continent to a place I'd never been. The car trip to Seattle alone would take at least eight hours and require two ferries. I would go from my quaint community with no stoplights and one gas station to a metropolis that included an interstate with multiple lanes, overpasses, and exits. The irony is that I'm the only person I know of who can get lost in a cul-de-sac. Get the picture?

You might be wondering, *If this trip scared her so much, why was she going in the first place?* Good question, and here's my answer: because God nudged me to go, I said yes. I agreed because I feared *him*. I respected him as God over all, and that included all of me. Besides, how could I *not* go when he had so obviously orchestrated the details?

For several months, I'd partnered with a friend to develop a line of greeting cards. I didn't know how to submit the idea to a publisher, so I searched for clues by googling a few key words. This was my first attempt at googling anything, and I had no idea what I was doing.

Results pointed me to the upcoming Florida Christian Writers Conference, where, wonder of wonders, an editor from my favorite greeting card publisher was on the faculty. *Wow! That conference sounds amazing*, I thought. Then came my inner naysayer: *But it's too far away. Florida is clear across the continent. Plus, I can't afford it. Not on our budget. And how can Gene and the kids survive without me for a week?*

That was August 1998. The naysayer's voice overruled, so I turned my focus to other things. A few months later in October, I attended a special church event where I had a catch-up conversation with one of the speakers' wives. Nineteen years earlier, she and I had graduated from the same Bible college. After learning that she worked as a travel agent, I asked for her phone number and told her I would give her a call if I ever took a trip.

Then November came. The thought of attending the conference returned, and this time it refused to be silenced. I knew in my heart of hearts that God was nudging me to go, so I asked my travel-agent friend to find the least expensive tickets.

She phoned a few hours later. "Give me your credit card info right now," she said. "I found round trip tickets for about $150. I've never seen such a good deal!" Thirty minutes later, a disclaimer appeared on her computer screen stating the price was a mistake, but all tickets purchased on that offer would be honored.

December arrived, and with it came the conference registration deadline. *How in the world am I going to pay the registration fee?* I fretted. It turns out God already had a plan for that too. When our family moved from Washington State to Quadra Island more than two years earlier, we had listed our house for sale, but the real estate market slowed to a trickle. Our home sat unsold … until that month. The sale provided funds for the registration fee.

Then January rolled around. A couple days before my departure, I still needed several hundred dollars to cover additional expenses. That's when a letter from our real estate agent arrived. Apparently someone in her office had made a math mistake when our house sold, and the oversight had shortchanged us financially. The letter included a check for the amount I lacked!

As I sat at the kitchen table in my mishmash of fear and anticipation, Gene gave my hand a gentle squeeze. "You'll be okay," he said. "God has a reason for you to attend this conference. He's got this. He is in control, and you can trust him."

Gene was right. Did God have a reason for me to attend the conference? Absolutely. It marked the beginning of the writing and teaching ministry I enjoy today.

Because God is El Elyon, he has the final say. We can trust him and live unafraid.

Was I okay, as Gene had predicted? Yes. In fact, I was better than okay. I not only made the trip and lived to tell the tale but also developed several lifelong friendships as a result.

Most importantly, the trip gave me the opportunity to experience God as *El Elyon*. It helped me see that he truly is in control of every detail of our lives. He has authority over all things, including Google key words, airline tickets, and yes, even math mistakes.

Because he is *El Elyon*, he has the final say. We can trust him and live unafraid.

El Elyon: What Does It Mean?

In the Bible, the Hebrew word *el* usually refers to the one true God or to a false god worshiped by the Canaanites, a nation that surrounded Israel. The Hebrew word *elyon* can be used as a descriptive word meaning "high" or "upper," but it is often used as a title that means "Highest" or "Most High," referring to God, monarchs, or angels.[1] The compound name *El Elyon* (pronounced "ehl ehl-YOHN") is translated as either "God Most High" or "Most High God," depending on the Bible version used.

Both the Israelites and Canaanites used this compound name. The Canaanites worshiped many gods but reserved *El Elyon* for the one they considered the highest in power. In contrast, the Israelites worshiped one God and acknowledged him as higher in rank, authority, and excellence than the false gods worshiped by surrounding nations.

The name *El Elyon* first appears in Genesis 14, when Abraham, or Abram—his name at the time—rescued Lot, his nephew. Four kings united to attack the kings who ruled in the area of Sodom and Gomorrah. They ransacked the cities and kidnapped many of the people there, including Lot. When Abram heard the news, he gathered his men, chased the marauders, and rescued the stolen goods and people.

A king and priest named Melchizedek met Abram upon his return and pronounced a blessing on him. Genesis 14:18 describes Melchizedek as "the king of Salem and a priest of God Most High [*El Elyon*]." He said to Abram, "Blessed be Abram by God Most High [*El Elyon*], Creator of heaven and earth. And blessed be God Most High [*El Elyon*], who has defeated your enemies for you" (verses 19–20).

Various forms of the name *El Elyon* appear throughout Scripture. One of the most familiar occurrences is in Psalm 91:1: "Those who live in the shelter of the Most High [*Elyon*] will find rest in the shadow of the Almighty." Perhaps you, like me and millions of other people around the world, find this verse reassuring.

Scary stuff comes our way, but fear need not consume us when we dwell in the presence of the all-supreme God who reigns over every detail of our lives. When we feel as though our world has gone crazy, we find courage in remembering that *El Elyon* remains in control:

> *Yours, O Lord, is the greatness, the power, the glory, the victory, and the majesty. Everything in the heavens and on earth is yours, O Lord, and this is your kingdom. We adore*

you as the one who is over all things. Wealth and honor come from you alone, for you rule over everything. Power and might are in your hand, and at your discretion people are made great and given strength.

1 CHRONICLES 29:11–12

When it seems like our lives are falling apart, we find peace in remembering that *El Elyon* has a plan: "Remember the things I have done in the past. For I alone am God! I am God, and there is none like me. Only I can tell you the future before it even happens. Everything I plan will come to pass, for I do whatever I wish" (Isaiah 46:9–10).

Many of the Bible's references to God as *Elyon* are reminiscent of the first of the Ten Commandments: "You shall have no other gods before me" (Exodus 20:3 NIV). Because God is highest in supremacy, it stands to reason that we give no thing or person precedence over him.

God's ultimate supremacy, sovereignty, and authority leave me in awe. Nothing compares to him. He is the Creator of heaven and earth, and there is no god more excellent, more magnificent, or higher in power.

El Elyon Is Supreme

One dictionary defines *supreme* as "highest in rank or authority; paramount; sovereign; chief"; "of the highest quality, degree, character, importance"; and "last or final, ultimate."[2] Numerous Bible verses declare God's supremacy. Here's just one example: "This is what the LORD says—Israel's King and Redeemer, the LORD of Heaven's Armies: 'I am the First and the Last; there is no other God'" (Isaiah 44:6). God knows no equivalent.

Are you familiar with the story in 1 Samuel 5 about Dagon, the Philistines' supreme deity? Touted as the father of the fertility god Baal, Dagon resembled a half-man, half-fish creature. People worshiped him for sending abundant harvests. When the Philistines captured the Ark of the Covenant from the Israelites, they brought it into Dagon's temple and placed it beside a statue of him. The townspeople arrived the next morning to find the idol on its face before the Ark (verses 2–3).

They set it back on its perch, but they found it face-down on the floor again the next morning. This time, Dagon's head and hands had broken off (verses 3–4). The Philistines' supreme deity literally couldn't stand in the presence of *El Elyon*, the one true God, highest in rank and authority.

This account reminds me of words written about Jesus—*El Elyon* in the flesh—in the apostle Paul's letter to the Philippians:

> God elevated him to the place of highest honor and gave him the name above all other names, that at the name of Jesus every knee should bow, in heaven and on earth and under the earth, and every tongue declare that Jesus Christ is Lord, to the glory of God the Father.

PHILIPPIANS 2:9-11

Chief. Ultimate. Paramount. That's *El Elyon*. And someday every man, woman, and child will bow their knees to him. When I think about being surrounded by his presence in heaven, I suspect that we will lower ourselves even further as awe and adoration compel us to drop to our faces before him.

El Elyon Is the Ultimate Authority

"In the beginning God created the heavens and the earth," says the first sentence in the Bible (Genesis 1:1). This verse is jam-packed with truth about who God is. He is the self-existent one, the Creator of everything that is. This role makes him the rightful owner of all he has made. Simply put, everything that *is*, is *his*.

El Elyon's ownership automatically gives him authority to do as he deems best with what belongs to him. Since he created the Red Sea, he held authority to part its waters, so the Israelites could escape from the Egyptian army (Exodus 14:13–28).

And that's not all. Because of God's creative authority,

- Manna (bread from heaven) covered the ground every morning, providing sustenance for the Israelites as they wandered in the wilderness for forty years (Exodus 16:35).

- The Jordan River stopped flowing, allowing Joshua to lead the Israelites, on dry land, into the Promised Land (Joshua 3:12–16).

- The sun stood still, allowing Israel enough daylight to defeat their enemies (Joshua 10:11–14).

- A whale swallowed Jonah and later spit him out, rescuing him from drowning in the sea (Jonah 1:17–2:10).

- Raging waters were calmed, rescuing Jesus and his disciples from the storm that threatened to sink the boat he and his disciples were sailing in (Matthew 8:23–27; Mark 4:35–41; Luke 8:22–25).

- A little boy's lunch was multiplied, feeding more than five thousand people (Matthew 14:13–21; Mark 6:31–44; Luke 9:12–17; John 6:1–14).

- Lazarus, a dead man, exited his tomb, foreshadowing Christ's resurrection (John 11:38–44).

God also has ultimate authority over we who profess Jesus as Savior, because he has bought us with his Son's shed blood (Ephesians 1:7). Ownership gives him authority to do with our lives as he deems best.

He might lead us to tackle tasks we wouldn't choose on our own. He might allow us to experience circumstances that bewilder or grieve us. But he will also allow these things to ultimately bless us in ways that far exceed our hopes and dreams.

When one of my friends was diagnosed with an advanced and aggressive form of cancer, people prayed for a miracle. She was a gifted writer and

Bible teacher, and we begged God to spare her life for the sake of her husband, kids, grandchildren, and ministry. But he said no.

My friend's death only five weeks post-diagnosis stunned everyone who knew her. I still can hardly believe she is no longer with us and wonder why God allowed this to happen. I have no answers, but I choose to accept *El Elyon*'s authority. He has purposes I don't understand, but this I know: His ways far outshine mine, because he is supreme in knowledge and wisdom.

El Elyon Is Sovereign

"God is the boss of everything," wrote David Wilkerson. "That means there are no accidents in my life—no such things as fate, happenstance or luck, either good or bad. Every step I take is ordered by the Lord. Everything in my life—in fact, everything in the universe—is under His control."[3]

Sometimes it might not feel like everything is under God's control, but it's true. I had to remind myself of this when Gene came home from work with the report that our newly hired office administrator had gone out to lunch and never returned. She later emailed to say that she quit because she felt overwhelmed.

The news floored me. Gene had fasted twice weekly for several months while praying for God to bring us the right person, and I did the same for a couple of months. Two of our ministry's board members joined Gene to interview this woman after she applied, and they all agreed that she appeared to be a good candidate. When offered the position, she accepted. On her third day of work, we enjoyed a staff lunch so everyone could get acquainted, and she fit in well.

She quit four days later.

My first response was, "You're kidding, right?" I admit feeling a tad annoyed with God for letting this happen when we desperately needed the help. And then I remembered what I'd been mulling over and writing about all day: God's sovereignty as manifested through the name *El Elyon*. Yup. I was working on this very session.

I don't believe in coincidences. God knew the disappointment we would face on that day, and he graciously arranged my writing schedule to coincide with it. He's up to something Gene and I can't see, and maybe we'll catch a glimpse of his purposes soon. Or maybe not.

Regardless, I'm hanging on to hope that comes from believing his sovereignty is alive and active and rules the day. One of my Bible college professors phrased it this way decades ago: "God is the blessed controller of all things." Her words gripped me in the classroom way back then, and I've recalled them countless times since in the classroom of life, especially when faced with grief or major disappointments.

> **El Elyon *is good, wise, and faithful. He is present. He is powerful. And we are beyond blessed to rest under his control.***

It's one thing to say that *El Elyon* controls the details of our lives—provided we let him—but it's another to call him "the *blessed* controller," especially when he allows suffering. Yet the truth remains: He knows what he's doing. Nothing catches him off guard. Nothing happens that he does not allow. Nothing baffles him, and nothing defeats him. He is good, wise, and faithful. He is present. He is powerful. And we are beyond blessed to rest under his control.

Abram Experiences God as *El Elyon*

Life's impossibilities are often the best places to discover fresh manifestations of God. Abram's rescue mission in Genesis 14 is no exception. From a human perspective, the odds were stacked against him.

When Abram learned that enemy armies had taken Lot and his family, he mustered his forces—a paltry 318 men. It's likely that each of the four armies he chased had several thousand troops, but even if each army went into battle with only the same number of men as Abram gathered, they still outnumbered his crew four to one.

The Genesis 14 account describes Abram's men as "trained" (verse 14), but they came from a line of nomadic herdsmen. Until this event, Abram had a reputation as a peace lover. Warring with enemy nations wasn't part of his history.

These fellows, all born into Abram's household, likely had lots of experience protecting their animals, but were they seasoned soldiers? How much experience did they have swinging swords in battle? How many times had they thrust a spear at an approaching enemy soldier? How often had they engaged in hand-to-hand combat? Even if they were adequately trained for war, the chances of 318 men defeating four armies were slim at best.

Despite the odds, Abram returned victorious. His accomplishment had nothing to do with military might or strategy. He won because *El Elyon* determined the outcome. As King of Kings and Lord of Lords, no one defeats his purposes or thwarts his plan.

Melchizedek met Abram upon his return from the battlefield. We know little about this man and his sudden appearance other than that he was the king of Salem—the original name for Jerusalem—and that he was a priest of the *Most High God* before the Levitical priesthood was established.

Most theologians agree that Melchizedek was a type, or foreshadowing, of Jesus. Melchizedek used the name *El Elyon* twice in his greeting and blessing, giving Abram an aha moment about God's character. We see evidence of this in Abram's response to the king of Sodom, who was also present and tried to strike a deal with him. "Give me the people and keep the goods," said the defeated king of Sodom (Genesis 14:21 NIV).

Keep in mind that the plunder included thousands of cows, goats, sheep, and camels. It glittered with gold and jewels. It contained household goods, clothing, and furniture. The loot might have lured a lesser man, but Abram wanted nothing to do with it. He rejected the offer and said, "I solemnly swear to the LORD, God Most High [*El Elyon*], Creator of heaven and earth, that I will not take so much as a single thread or sandal thong from what belongs to you. Otherwise you might say, 'I am the one who made Abram rich'" (Genesis 14:22–23).

Melchizedek's usage of the name *El Elyon* opened Abram's spiritual eyes to see God as the Creator and, therefore, the rightful owner of everything in existence. Considering this revelation, the plunder was nothing more than a collection of trinkets that wasn't his to keep anyway.

The name *El Elyon* also reminded Abram that God's sovereignty was responsible for his victory over the enemy kings. Abram's vow demonstrated his desire to ensure credit was given where credit was due.

The manifestation of God as *El Elyon* elevated Abram's faith to a new level. I like to think this aha moment played a role in his response when, years later, God told him to sacrifice his son Isaac. Abram didn't argue or try to dissuade God from this bewildering command. The morning after receiving it, he packed up and headed out.

We can only imagine the thoughts he entertained as he hiked up the mountain on the last leg of his journey. *I will trust and obey* El Elyon, *the* Most High God, *because of who he is. I've seen his sovereignty rule over impossible circumstances in the past, and I believe he will do it again.*

I have no doubt that catching a glimpse of God's supremacy led to Abram's surrendering to his authority. And rightfully so. He's the boss, and we are not. Trouble is, we sometimes forget who's in charge.

Turning this attitude around is imperative if we hope to move from fear to freedom. Some of us figure it out and step back to let God step up, but others? Well, they need a little nudge to let go and let God have his way.

Carole's Story: Surrendered and Equipped

Conversation ran deep as Carole Lewis and I walked down a Texas country road early one morning. We were attending a First Place for Health wellness retreat, and she was the ministry's national director at the time.

I'd met her only the day before, but I loved her already and knew she was someone I could consider a mentor. She radiated love for Jesus and his Word. Her countenance reflected peace, and the sparkle in her eyes revealed joy. I assumed that Carole had enjoyed a carefree, pain-free life, but I soon discovered my assumption was wrong.

As Carole related her story, I learned that she and her husband, Johnny, were forced to declare bankruptcy when the economic downturn in the mid-1980s dried up their forklift business almost overnight. State law allowed them to keep their house and furnishings, but they lost their car and savings. As difficult as it was, this event would change her life for the better.

Carole had placed her faith in Jesus for salvation as a twelve-year-old, but thirty years had passed without her acknowledging his authority. She feared that doing so would give God permission to do something like—heaven forbid—send her to China or Africa as a missionary. If he didn't send *her*, then he'd probably send her kids, and she didn't want them to live so far from home. Confident that she'd go to heaven if she died, Carole was content to sit on the throne of her life and relegate God to the back quarters.

"I was a carnal Christian," Carole remarked. "God did not have all of me. I pretty much went through life saying, 'God, you take care of heaven, and I'll look after things on earth. I'll call you if I have a problem.'"

After their business failed, Carole was still trying to manage on her own—until one Sunday morning, when she listened to her pastor preach about the human will.

"God is a perfect gentleman," said the pastor. "He won't barge in and work on your stubborn will without your permission. If you don't want to surrender to his way today, then I encourage you to pray, 'God, I'm not willing, but I'm willing to be made willing.'"

By that time, the bankruptcy had pushed Carole to desperation. She made that prayer her own, but still fearing what God might do if she yielded to his authority, she added a postscript: "Please don't let it hurt too bad." Immediately, God began to manifest himself as *El Elyon*.

First came his sovereign hand in her job situation. She never attended college because she had married after high school and then given birth to three children in four years. But her lack of a degree didn't hinder *El Elyon*. Carole saw his hand when she got a job in her church office and was soon promoted to a supervisory position. Later she became assistant director of the Wellness Center at her church, which involved overseeing women's ministries and the First Place for Health program.

When Carole surrendered to God's authority, she never imagined that through her leadership, he would grow First Place for Health from fifty participating churches to twelve hundred. Six months later, she was promoted to the full-time role of national director.

Through that ministry, God brought into Carole's life two women whose passion for Scripture memory inspired and challenged her to memorize one hundred verses over the next two years. Her love for God's Word and her friendship with him deepened as a result. Carole later realized how, in his sovereignty, *El Elyon* had orchestrated these circumstances to prepare her for a difficult road ahead.

First, Carole's beloved Johnny was diagnosed with stage four prostate cancer. Then her elderly mother, wheelchair-bound and suffering with dementia, moved in and stayed with them for the last three and a half years of her life.

On Thanksgiving evening, 2001, a drunk driver struck Carole's thirty-nine-year-old daughter, Shari, as she stood in her in-laws' yard. Shari was rushed into surgery but died on the operating table. She left behind her husband and three daughters.

In 2008, Hurricane Ike brought a seventeen-foot tidal surge that demolished Carole and Johnny's home on the bay. Johnny—who had outlived his doctor's prediction—died several years later. Six months after his passing, cancer claimed Shari's widower and orphaned Carole's three granddaughters.

Carole could have dwelt on her tragedies, but she chose to focus on God's sovereignty in them. Losing her home on the bay is one example. She and Johnny considered rebuilding but decided instead to live near family in Houston. Soon afterward, First Place for Health, headquartered in Houston, underwent significant changes that required her undivided time and attention. Thanks to *El Elyon*, she was already local and able to be fully present. And when Johnny's health declined, their new living situation provided easy access for family members to visit and lend a hand.

In the days following Shari's death, Carole wrote down every event in which she saw God at work. For instance, two women volunteered to clean house and prepare meals for Shari's family. He provided a caregiver for Carole's mom so Carole could focus on Shari's family and funeral service. He even encouraged Shari's oldest daughter by sending an anticipated college acceptance letter the morning after the accident.

"Thinking I had control of my life for those thirty years was the silliest thing, but that's where I was," said Carole. "God used bankruptcy to get me to the place where he wanted me to be: surrendered and content to live under his authority."

We might read Carole's story and think, *She was right to believe that giving God control of her life would be scary. After all, look at all the bad stuff that happened.* But let's reframe our perspective, lest our thoughts head down the wrong path. Consider this statement by the late Bible teacher and author Jerry Bridges:

That which should distinguish the suffering of believers from unbelievers is the confidence that our suffering is under the control of an all-powerful and all-loving God; our suffering has meaning and purpose in God's eternal plan, and He brings or allows to come into our lives only that which is for His glory and our good.[4]

Carole would agree. Surrendering to God's supremacy put her on a journey that prepared her for hardships he knew lay ahead. Being prepared, in turn, helped her not only survive but also thrive when those hardships hit. She learned rich lessons that she has been able to share with others through her books and Bible-teaching ministry, and the outcome has given God the glory he deserves. Yielding to God's authority didn't bring on Carole's suffering; it equipped her and carried her through.

It also transformed her.

When Carole yielded her will to God that Sunday morning, he began to change her from the inside out. In earlier days, she'd written a list of all the things she would happily do for God and those she would not. "But he switched those lists," Carole said. "Today I'm doing everything I said I wouldn't be able to do nor want to do, and I'm absolutely loving it."

I know what you're wondering. No, God didn't send Carole to China or Africa. Neither did he send her kids.

Submitting to *El Elyon's* supremacy doesn't mean he'll make us do what we fear and dread most. It means he changes our desires, dreams, and goals to align with *his* desires, dreams, and goals for us. But we must first be willing to let him have first place in our hearts.

What we habitually think about God and his ways is of utmost importance. Continually entertaining thoughts that he wants to make us miserable will create a stubborn resistance toward him, but accurate thoughts centered on how he is wise and good and wants our best will help us surrender to him. The more accurate our thinking, the more willing we will be to acknowledge his supremacy, and the more we will enjoy an ever-deepening relationship with him as we seek to live unafraid.

How Shall We Respond?

Because God is supreme in every conceivable way, he deserves our immediate and enthusiastic surrender to his authority. Unfortunately, we tend to do the opposite.

It started way back in the beginning, when the angel Lucifer, or Satan, determined in his heart to exalt himself above other created beings and make himself equal with God. "I will climb to the highest heavens and be like the Most High," he said to himself (Isaiah 14:14). Pride resulted in his falling from heaven, and he has been inciting mankind to join his rebellion ever since.

God does not take it lightly when we exalt our wants and wishes above his desires and directives for us.

After God commanded Adam and Eve not to eat from one specific tree in the garden of Eden, they could have complied and enjoyed fruit from all the other trees— but no. Eve doubted God's intent toward them, and she and her husband elevated their desires above God's authority when they agreed with the serpent's (Satan's) lies. Their sin separated them from God's presence and led to death (Genesis 3).

King Nebuchadnezzar's pride landed him in a pasture, where he lost his mind and lived with wild animals for seven years. God humbled him "so that everyone may know that the Most High rules over the kingdoms of the world. He gives them to anyone he chooses—even to the lowliest of people" (Daniel 4:17).

God does not take it lightly when we exalt our wants and wishes above his desires and directives for us. He is God, and we are not; and this order will remain throughout eternity. Let's make our earthly existence a dress rehearsal for heaven by giving him the honor he deserves here and now.

How can we do this?

First, let's invite the Holy Spirit to show us where we have slighted God through proud thoughts, words, and actions. Maybe we've refused to accept a divine assignment that feels risky. Perhaps we've disregarded his directive to forgive an offender or to show unconditional love to someone who grates on our nerves. Maybe we've ignored his commands to give thanks in all circumstances, give generously, and show kindness to strangers in our land. Or it's possible that we've become so full of ourselves that there's no room left for the Holy Spirit to fill us.

When the Spirit pinpoints our sin, let's neither deny nor justify it. Let's agree with him, confess our shortcomings, and receive forgiveness and a fresh start.

Next, let's ask the Holy Spirit to show us if we've set any other gods before the one true God. Granted, in our culture, we're not likely worshiping idols made of wood or stone. We do, however, bow the knee to gods like money, material possessions, sports, social media, physical appearance, food, work, hobbies, sex, security, power, position, and public image.

Let's pause here, okay? Read that list again ... slowly and thoughtfully. On which of these modern-day gods have you lavished your attention? Which ones have stolen your heart? Be honest with yourself and with the Lord, because he knows all about it anyway. This isn't news to him.

Before moving on, commit to restoring God to first place. Ask him to teach you how to love him as he deserves—with all your heart, soul, mind, and strength (Matthew 22:36-40; Mark 12:28-31; Luke 10:27). He will answer your prayer in the affirmative, I guarantee.

Finally, let's commit to trusting God's sovereignty in our lives. I know, I know—easier said than done. We say we trust him, his wisdom, and his ways, but our desire to be in control says otherwise. We think we know the best outcome and how to achieve it, but we're only kidding ourselves. "Most Christians salute the sovereignty of God but believe in the sovereignty of man," said R. C. Sproul.[5]

Let's resolve to not be counted in the majority. "God owes us no explanation for what He does and why He does it," says Bob Jennerich. "We wouldn't understand His explanation anyway. God's thoughts are above ours. Explaining them to us is like us trying to teach algebra to a dog."[6]

When things happen beyond your understanding, resist the temptation to demand a divine explanation. Instead, ask God to reveal the lessons he wants you to learn through those circumstances. Focus on the truth that he is good and wise and has your best interest in mind.

Our souls crave peace. Our hearts long to live unafraid. Knowing God by his name *El Elyon* satisfies those desires. He is working out his purposes, both on a global scale and for each of us individually. He is supreme, he is sovereign, and he has the final say. He's got this, and everything is going to be okay.

Prayer

El Elyon, I praise you for being the supreme God who is sovereign over all. You are God of heaven and earth, and there is none like you. I surrender my desire to be in charge and yield to your control. I invite you to reshape my stubborn will and align it with your perfect will. I resolve to trust your wisdom and unfailing love when you allow me to experience difficult circumstances. Throughout each day, open my eyes to see evidence of your sovereignty and ultimate authority, and teach me to rest in it. Help me walk in the truth of this manifestation of your character, and transform me through the process. In Jesus's name, amen.

Points TO *Ponder*

1 Read Psalm 112:1.

- What does it mean to "fear the LORD?"

- Based on what you've learned in this study, why does God deserve our respect?

- Describe the attitude with which we're to obey him.

- How can understanding God by his name *El Elyon* help us obey him with this kind of attitude?

2 Read 1 Samuel 2:6-10.

- How does this passage demonstrate God's sovereignty?

- Over what does he rule?

- How do these words encourage you today?

3 Read Job 1:6-12.

- This passage provides insight into Satan's relationship to God's sovereignty. Who is in charge? Identify the clues that indicate this to be true.

- Compare this passage with Acts 16:16-17. What title for God did the evil spirit use?

- How does knowing that God is the boss give us courage when we feel afraid?

4 Read Genesis 45:5, 7-8; 50:20.

- After Joseph's brothers sold him into slavery, his master's wife falsely accused him of sexual assault. He spent years in an Egyptian prison as a result. How did Joseph respond?

- How does his example reframe your perspective toward difficult circumstances in your life?

5 Read 1 Thessalonians 5:18.

■ How does understanding God as *El Elyon* empower us to give thanks in every situation?

■ Identify a challenge you're currently facing, and take a moment to thank God for his sovereignty over it.

Scan the QR code or go to

hendricksonrose.org/ LivingUnafraidSession7

for more author insights about the name *El Elyon*.

Afterword

Every book I write brings a battle of its own, but *Living Unafraid* brought more than one. The fear of inadequacy came first. *Who are you to write this book?* it taunted.

The fear of failure followed. I faced an impending deadline to submit my manuscript, but an important family need required my attention for seven weeks. Each day brought me closer to the deadline. Fear whispered, *There's no way you're going to finish this book on time.*

Fearing that my family's well-being was at risk also loomed large. While I stayed with my daughter for those seven weeks to help her through a difficult pregnancy, my husband learned that his prostate cancer had grown more aggressive. Performing due diligence to determine the most appropriate treatment became a priority.

The fear of financial insecurity cast its shadow when our car's transmission blew in the middle of all that was happening. Our trusty mechanic said a new transmission for this model would cost $12,000—a number far beyond our budget. Besides that, we're a single-car family, and our ministry office is an hour's drive from home. How would my husband get to and from work until we could find a solution?

When I finally sat down to focus on the book, I faced a string of events that felt like personal attacks: An eye infection. Mouth sores. A foot injury that landed me in an air boot for six weeks. A close-call car accident. A freak fall on my boat-home. An invisible target on my back flashed like a neon sign: "Hit me! Hit me!"

I suspect the enemy wanted me to curl into a fetal position and forget about writing, but I could not—would not—give him the upper hand. A year earlier, I'd developed material about the names of God for a Zoom Bible study, and the truths I discovered were life-giving. I felt compelled to delve deeper and share what I had learned so others could experience the freedom and joy I'd discovered. The more I dug into this topic and God's Word, the more treasures I unearthed. Throughout the process of writing, I experienced the manifestations of God's names in so many ways that I was left with no choice but to live unafraid.

Yahweh reminded me that, yes, he is the almighty Creator of heaven and earth, but he's never too busy to lend an ear or a helping hand. What an honor to be constantly in his thoughts and close to his heart.

Yahweh Tzidkenu reassured me that he loves me because I'm his child, not because I'm an author. It's easy to feel pressured to produce a winning manuscript, but *Yahweh Tzidkenu* released me from that stress by reminding me to write for his pleasure.

Yahweh Rohi led me past mental roadblocks on the days I felt stumped. He made me lie down beside still waters (literally) and refreshed my soul when I felt weary. He calmed my fears about my husband's health and led us to a skilled oncologist who helped us determine the best course of treatment.

Yahweh Yireh provided energy to rise early every day so I could spend quiet moments in his presence. He provided time to write. The book aside, he even provided our mechanic with a good used transmission within our budget.

Yahweh Tzevaot helped me wield the sword of truth in response to the enemy's taunts about this project and my family's well-being. Fear could not prevail in the presence of *The Lord of Hosts*.

Yahweh Shammah came alongside and enveloped me with a sense of his sweet and powerful presence. He used worship songs, Bible verses, and friends' encouraging emails to remind me that he was with me.

Finally, *El Elyon* reminded me that he is the ultimate authority over heaven and earth. Nothing stops him from accomplishing his purposes; therefore, I could trust him to help me write this book.

And he did. In fact, he enabled me to submit the manuscript a month before the deadline! I know this was his doing, since there is no human explanation for how it happened.

I am forever grateful for the opportunity to have authored *Living Unafraid*, because the process has changed my life. The truths I discovered along the way have sparked a spiritual revival. They have caused me to renew my surrender to the God who is completely wise, good, and trustworthy. They leave me breathless in awe and wonder that he loves and cares for me. And they compel me to bow my head and bend my knees in worship before him who is worthy of all praise.

My prayer for you, dear reader, is that you will allow *Living Unafraid* to spark a revival in your heart too. Choose now to bow to the only one worthy of your adoration. Invite him to give you opportunities to experience him by name. Ask him to open your eyes to his magnificence. Place your surrendered heart in his nail-pierced hands, and experience the joy of moving from fear to freedom.

Please feel free to connect with me. I'd love to hear your story. How has understanding God's character as manifested through his names made a difference in your life?

Know you are loved,

Grace

gracefox.com
grace@gracefox.com

Acknowledgments

It takes a team to bring any book to publication, and I'm grateful for every individual who worked behind the scenes to place this book in readers' hands.

Lynnette Pennings—thank you for listening as I shared thoughts on writing about God's names when we met over lunch at that little restaurant in Iowa. Thanks, too, for encouraging me to submit a proposal and for waiting patiently until I produced it. You're a stellar managing editor, and your faith in me spurs me onward.

Anisa Larramore—thanks for using your editorial brilliance to make this book the best it could be. And thank you for praying over it with me. Partnering with you is sheer joy.

Jon Bryant, thank you for lending your Hebrew expertise and biblical and theological knowledge to help ensure accuracy.

Elizabeth Wingate—I appreciate the editorial skills you also brought to the project. Another set of eyes is always a good thing before sending a book to print.

John Ribeiro—I owe heartfelt thanks for the support you've shown as my publisher. Your faith in me inspires me to excellence, and your generosity sends this message of living unafraid to far corners of the world.

Cristalle Kishi, Sergio Urquiza, Dave Pietrantonio, and Anestis Jordanoglou—your creative genius and production support makes *Living Unafraid* a beauty to behold and a joy to read.

Caleb Weston—your techie genius leaves me in awe. Thank you for making the videos shine and for doing everything necessary to make them available to our readers.

Raechel Wong, Glen Andrews, and everyone involved in sales and marketing—I owe you a huge load of thanks for promoting *Living Unafraid* far and wide. I appreciate you and your desire to see people walk in freedom from fear.

My dear readers—you responded when I posted online pleas for prayer. I know your prayers made a difference.

And last but certainly not least—Gene, my husband and best friend—you're the wind beneath my wings. Your ongoing encouragement and prayers carried me to the finish line. So did your servant's heart. Thanks for doing the laundry and cooking dinner on days when the deadline loomed large. And thanks for walking this faith journey with me. You're my one and only.

Notes

SESSION 1
Yahweh—I am who I am

1. See footnote on Exodus 3:14 NLT.
2. Tony Evans, *The Power of God's Names* (Eugene, OR: Harvest House, 2014), 46.
3. Rita Schulte, *Shattered: Finding Hope and Healing through the Losses of Life* (Abilene, TX: Leafwood, 2013), 94.
4. Evans, *The Power of God's Names*, 51.
5. Michael L. Gowens, *A Study of God's Hebrew Names* (Shallotte, NC: Sovereign Grace, 2016), 59.

SESSION 2
Yahweh Tzidkenu—The Lord Is Our Righteousness

1. *Blue Letter Bible*, s.v. "Strong's H6664— ṣeḏeq," *https://www.blueletterbible.org /lexicon/h6664/niv/wlc/0-1/.*
2. *The American Heritage Dictionary of the English Language*, 2022, s.v. "righteous," *https://ahdictionary.com/word/search.html?q=righteousness.*
3. Learn more about Donna Farrar at *https://www.donnasherrie.com.*
4. Tchiki Davis, "Shame: Definition, Causes, and Tips," *Berkeley Well-Being Institute: https://www.berkeleywellbeing.com/shame.html.*
5. Craig Groeschel, *The Christian Atheist: Believing in God but Living as if He Doesn't Exist* (Grand Rapids, MI: Zondervan, 2010), 50.
6. Tony Evans, *The Power of God's Names* (Eugene, OR: Harvest House, 2014), 171–72.
7. Craig Groeschel, *Soul Detox: Clean Living in a Contaminated World* (Grand Rapids, MI: Zondervan, 2012), 226.

SESSION 3
Yahweh Rohi—The Lord Is My Shepherd

1. *Bible Study Tools*, s.v. "Ra`ah,"*https://www.biblestudytools.com/lexicons/hebrew/nas /raah-3.html.*
2. *Blue Letter Bible*, s.v. "Strong's H7462—rāʿâ," *https://www.blueletterbible.org /lexicon/h7462/kjv/wlc/0-1/.*
3. A. W. Tozer, *The Knowledge of the Holy* (San Francisco: Harper and Brothers, 1961), 66.

4. Thomas O. Chisholm, "Great Is Thy Faithfulness," from *Psalms and Hymns to the Living God*, 185, *Hymnary.org*: *https://hymnary.org/text/great_is_thy_faithfulness_o_god_my_fathe*.

5. David Wilkerson, *Knowing God by Name: Names of God That Bring Hope and Healing* (Grand Rapids, MI: Chosen Books, 2003), 149.

6. Skip Moen, "Face Time," October 22, 2006, *Hebrew Word Study | Skip Moen: https://skipmoen.com/2006/10/face-time-2/*.

7. *Blue Letter Bible*, s.v. "Strong's H6887—ṣārar," *https://www.blueletterbible.org/lexicon/h6887/nlt/wlc/0-1/*. See also Skip Moen, "What Binds Me," October 24, 2006, *Hebrew Word Study | Skip Moen: https://skipmoen.com/2006/10/what-binds-me/*.

SESSION 4
Yahweh Yireh—The LORD Will Provide

1. David Wilkerson, *Knowing God by Name: Names of God That Bring Hope and Healing* (Grand Rapids, MI: Chosen Books, 2003), 26.

2. *Blue Letter Bible*, s.v. "Strong's H7200—rā'â," *https://www.blueletterbible.org/lexicon/h7200/nlt/wlc/0-1/*.

3. Max Lucado, *Fearless: Imagine Your Life without Fear* (Nashville: Thomas Nelson, 2009), 50.

4. Visit Cyndi Wilkens's website at *https://cyndisstory.com* to learn more about her story and her book, *Shine On* (Winnipeg, MB: Word Alive, 2017).

5. Craig Groeschel, *Twitter, https://twitter.com/craiggroeschel/status/567007118998269953* (February 15, 2015, 12:06 p.m.).

6. Max Lucado, *Just like Jesus: A Heart like His* (Nashville: Thomas Nelson, 2003), 53.

7. Jennifer Kennedy Dean, *Prized: Experience the Tender Love of the Savior* (Birmingham, AL: New Hope, 2019), 56.

SESSION 5
Yahweh Tzevaot—The LORD of Hosts

1. George Stein, "Hannah: A Case of Infertility and Depression," *British Journal of Psychiatry* 197, no. 6 (December 2010):492, *doi.org/10.1192/bjp.197.6.492*.

2. Charles R. Swindoll, *Perfect Trust* (Nashville: J. Countryman, 2000), 69.

3. Tony Evans, *The Power of God's Names* (Eugene, OR: Harvest House, 2014), 78.

4. Learn more about Deb Gruelle at *debgruelle.com*.

5. Christine Caine, interview by Jonathan Petersen, *Bible Gateway Blog*, November 21, 2017, *https://biblegateway.com/blog/2017/11/how-to-find*

-unshakeable-strength-in-the-bible-an-interview-with-christine-caine/.

6. To learn more about the First Place for Health ministry, visit *First Place for Health: https://www.firstplaceforhealth.com*.

7. R. C. Sproul, *The Holiness of God* (Carol Stream, IL: Tyndale Momentum, 2020), 36.

8. Sproul, *The Holiness of God*, 36.

SESSION 6
Yahweh Shammah—The LORD Is There

1. Gift Gugu Mona, *Daily Quotes about God: 365 Days of Heavenly Inspiration* (Hazyview, South Africa: Precious Gift Consulting, 2019), 79. Used with permission.

2. Terry Law with Jim Gilbert, *The Power of Praise and Worship* (Shippensburg, PA: Destiny Image, 2008), 145.

3. Learn more about Dawn Damon's ministry at *http://www.dawnscottdamon.com*.

4. C. S. Lewis, *Letters to Malcolm: Chiefly on Prayer* (New York: Harcourt, Brace & World, 1964), 75.

5. Thomas Keating, *Open Mind, Open Heart: The Contemplative Dimension of the Gospel* (New York: Continuum, 2006), 34.

6. Max Lucado, *God Will Carry You Through* (Nashville: Thomas Nelson, 2013), 41.

7. Brother Lawrence, *The Practice of the Presence of God* (New Kensington, PA: Whitaker House, 1982), 61.

SESSION 7
El Elyon—Most High God

1. *Bible Hub*, s.v. "5945—Elyown," *https://biblehub.com/hebrew/5945.htm*.

2. *Dictionary.com*, s.v. "supreme," *https://www.dictionary.com/browse/supreme*.

3. David Wilkerson, *Knowing God by Name: Names of God That Bring Hope and Healing* (Grand Rapids, MI: Chosen Books, 2003), 19.

4. Jerry Bridges, *Trusting God* (Colorado Springs: NavPress, 2008), 239–40.

5. R. C. Sproul, "Who's Truly Sovereign?" *Ultimately* (podcast), September 6, 2021, *Ligonier Ministries, https://www.ligonier.org/podcasts/ultimately-with-rc-sproul/whos-truly-sovereign*.

6. Bob Jennerich, *Facing Life's Challenges Head On: How Jesus Gets You Through What You Can't Get Around* (2021), chapter 3: "Doubt," section: "The Reason for Doubt," para. 4.

More from Grace Fox

A diagnosis. Death of a loved one. A layoff. A broken relationship. Life changes in a nanosecond when storms sweep in, often without warning. They leave our knuckles white and our hearts broken. With minds barely able to think clearly, we often set our Bible aside. In reality, that's when we need its comfort and strength most. These devotionals are written for those in crisis, for those longing for hope but lacking the ability to focus on a lengthy Scripture passage. These minute-sized devotions offer respite to readers caught in the storms of life.

KEEPING HOPE ALIVE
Devotions for Strength in the Storm

ISBN: 978-1-64938-051-7

FINDING HOPE IN CRISIS
Devotions to Calm the Chaos

ISBN: 978-1-62862-992-7

FRESH HOPE FOR TODAY
Devotions for Joy on the Journey

ISBN: 978-1-64938-055-5

www.hendricksonrose.com